ARTHUR PLOTNIK

SPUNK

& BITE

A Writer's Guide to Punchier, More Engaging Language & Style

RANDOM HOUSE REFERENCE
New York   Toronto   London   Sydney   Auckland

Library of Congress Cataloging-in-Publication Data

Plotnik, Arthur.
    Spunk & bite : a writer's guide to punchier, more engaging language & style / Arthur Plotnik.
        p. cm.
    Includes index.
    ISBN 0-375-72115-0
    1. Authorship. 2. English language—Rhetoric. 3. English language—Style. I. Title: Spunk and bite. II. Title.

PN147.P55 2005

808'.042—dc22   2005044934

Visit the Random House Reference Web site: *www.randomwords.com*.

ISBN: 0-375-72115-0

Printed in the United States of America

10   9   8   7   6   5   4   3   2   1

CONTENTS

INTRODUCTION   *vii*

Flexibility / A LITTLE LIGHT UNSTRUNKTION

ONE / E. B. Whitewashed: A Starting Point   *2*

Freshness / THE WALLOP OF THE NEW

TWO / The Pleasures of Surprise   *10*

THREE / Extreme Expression   *16*

FOUR / Writers' Words, Drop by Dottle   *23*

FIVE / Upgrading Your Colors   *30*

SIX / Joltingly Fresh Adverbs   *37*

Texture / WRITING INTO THE MOOD

SEVEN / Tense: A Sticky Choice   *44*

EIGHT / Diction: We Are the Words   *53*

NINE / The Punchy Trope   *61*

Word / LANGUAGE—AEROBATIC AND INCANDESCENT

TEN / How to Loot a Thesaurus   72

ELEVEN / Words with Music and *Sploosh*   80

TWELVE / Coining the *Bonne* Locution   86

THIRTEEN / Words with Foreign *Umami*   93

Force / STIMULATION BY ANY MEANS

FOURTEEN / Dialogue Tags with Oomph   106

FIFTEEN / Enallage: A Fun Grammatical Get   113

SIXTEEN / Intensifiers for the Feeble   120

SEVENTEEN / Opening Words: The Glorious Portal   127

EIGHTEEN / Closings: The Three-Point Landing   140

Form / LIFE BETWEEN THE MARKS

NINETEEN / The Joys of Hyper-Hyphenation   148

TWENTY / A License. To Fragment. Sentences.   155

TWENTY-ONE / The Poetry of Lists   163

TWENTY-TWO / The Art of the Semicolon   171

TWENTY-THREE / Daringly Quoteless Dialogue   180

Clarity / "A HOUSE OF GREAT SPICKNESS AND SPANNESS"

TWENTY-FOUR / The Feng Shui of Writing   188

TWENTY-FIVE / Hunting Down Danglers *196*

TWENTY-SIX / Magic in the Names of Things *205*

TWENTY-SEVEN / The Earnestly Engaging Sentence *213*

Contemporaneity / A LEG UP ON THE COMPETITION

TWENTY-EIGHT / Writing for New Generations *224*

TWENTY-NINE / Hot Pop and Ephemeragy *234*

THIRTY / Edge: Writing at the Nervy Limits *242*

THIRTY-ONE / Parting Words: Butterflies
in the Killing Fields *250*

INDEX *255*

PERMISSIONS/ACKNOWLEDGMENTS

With gratitude I acknowledge the kind permission of Elena Karina Byrne for use of lines from her poem, "Sex Mask," as it appeared in *Chelsea 76;* and of Christina A. Thompson (*Harvard Review*), John Tait (*American Literary Review*), and Ronald Spatz (*Alaska Review*) for remarks they provided for an earlier article of mine.

For other helpful kindnesses, I thank Elfrieda M. Abbe and Jeff Reich of *The Writer* magazine; the reference staff of the Chicago Public Library; friends and former colleagues at the American Library Association; Sean Morris, Ilene Cooper, Rudy Joenk, and William Meehan; agent Ed Knappman and editor Jena Pincott; support team Plotnik/Taub; and my constant advisor and soul mate, Mary Phelan.

Portions of some chapters appeared, in earlier versions, in *The Writer* magazine and *The Editorial Eye* newsletter. —A.P.

ALSO BY ARTHUR PLOTNIK

The Elements of Editing

The Man Behind the Quill: Jacob Shallus, Calligrapher
of the United States Constitution

The Elements of Authorship

The Elements of Expression

The Urban Tree Book

INTRODUCTION

Sometimes when I'm digging for the right word, I long for a terrier-like acuity, a canine's sensory gifts applied to language. Imagine if dogs ever figured out how to write—how to put that spunkiness and bite of theirs into literature. Think of those olfactory superpowers attuned to sniffing out metaphors or tracking, not the bone *mot,* but the *bon mot.* We dry-and-fleshy-nosed writers could be in big trouble.

Some of us are there anyway. With so many gifted authors already sniffing their way to publication, with so many diversions grabbing mass attention, no writer can afford a writing-as-usual attitude. Language or style that is less engaging, less stimulating than the competition is, frankly, dead on arrival. Whether you strive as a journalist, novelist, poet, copywriter, corporate communicator, student—or even as a yearning presence on Match.com—something distinctive, some *umami*-like deliciousness has to emanate from your words or off they go to oblivion. Most writers feel themselves on the scent of such expressiveness, but just a few bounds short of seizing it. In this book, I've done my best to help close that distance without losing the fun of the chase.

Looking at all types of contemporary writing, *Spunk & Bite* distills the elements that make for punch and vibrancy; it identifies successful techniques and tricks of the trade, including those spurned by conventional guides; and it illustrates its advice with brief, sparking examples from our best writers.

Although it occasionally tweaks "correctness" to the times, *Spunk & Bite* is not another Strunk & White—as the iconic writer's rule book *Elements of Style* is known; instead, it addresses those whose basic composition skills are as adequate as the next writer's, but who itch for creative ideas, smart locutions, and realistic takes on language for today's media.

Not that I myself claim a hound's quickness in getting the prize between my jaws; but I do have one special gift, perhaps the odd fruit of a life as editor, author, and reader:

I can see dead writing.

I see language that follows all the rules, but lacks the vigor and inventiveness ever to rise off the page. It talks to me; keens over what it has learned too late, pleads that I pass these lessons on to the hopeful.

I feel the anguish of dead writing, and sometimes as an editor I've applied a stitch here, a jolt there, so that it might stagger among the undead. But the only authentic way to enliven a piece of writing, give it corporeal clout, is to invigorate it at the outset. To this end, *Spunk & Bite* fosters some unorthodox approaches; it is not, however, about out-shrieking the next writer or trashing the language authorities. Its observations and advice (to be read in order or, after Chapter one, randomly) are meant to energize writing and liberate it from certain outdated style conventions.

Of course, throwing off restraints is one thing; deciding what to do with that freedom is another. Will it be to create self-indulgent drivel, or adventurous art that engages editors and readers? If you aspire to the latter, if you write to get published and heard—or if you simply enjoy the pursuit of vivid language—then this spunky dog will hunt, I tell you, or I'm a French poodle.

—*A.P., Chicago*

INTRODUCTION

Flexibility

A LITTLE LIGHT UNSTRUNKTION

ONE
E. B. WHITEWASHED:
A STARTING POINT

Place yourself in the background. Do not affect a breezy manner. Do not inject opinion. Use figures of speech sparingly. Avoid foreign languages. Prefer the standard to the offbeat.

What have we here—a gulag for deviant writers? Whenever I review those dictates from *The Elements of Style,* that cynosure of American composition by William Strunk Jr. and E. B. White, I feel I should make a dash for it, vault the gates into the free zone.

In the course of a long writing career, I have often been on the lam from Composition 101 and its constables, Strunk and White. After all, I *want* my opinion heard. I *want* to be offbeat. What writer doesn't? I want to be so offbeat that crazed readers chase me down alleys. And yet I keep staggering back to *The Elements of Style* to review those sensible rules I want to savage—or embrace—in my next piece.

Schizoid? Not given the yin-and-yangness of today's readership: half focused, half distracted; half in the armchair savoring the well-chosen word, half seeking thrills in the electronic wilds. Somehow the writer must flag attention in a swirl of divergent moods, trends, and affinities. If the idea of writing is indeed to be published and read, then writers want flexibility. They want both sheriff *and* outlaw roaming those right brains to rein in the yang

[2]

SPUNK & BITE

or conspire with the yin. Of course, in brains attuned to the *The Elements of Style,* the sheriff is already on the scene—and he is one puissant little cuss. Just about every writer of American prose feels Strunk and White's tug. How astonishing that this diminutive book has maintained such a hold on our writing. How did this happen? How is it justified? Which of Strunk and White's teachings should writers respect? And which should they rebel against?

As an author of writing advice, I've tried repeatedly to answer such questions to my own satisfaction. And whenever I think I've done so, new waves of adulation for *Elements of Style* dampen my convictions. But one thing stays with me: Each time I return to Strunk and White's otherwise purehearted classic, I discover what I can only describe as a certain troublesome whitewash in their approach. And though I'm not the only one to have discovered it, I'm the only one who's going to tell you about it here and now, for your own good!

RULES VS USAGE: THE WARRING SIDES

Pound for pound, no American writing guide is more revered than the five-ounce *Elements of Style,* aka Strunk and White. No reference book sells more copies or draws gushier superlatives (*Timeless!; Nonpareil!; The best book of its kind!*). With some ten million copies rooted on as many reference shelves, Strunk and White has become the ivy (if not the kudzu) on our great walls of clarity and correctness.

Yet for all its glory, the book can be a magnet for bashers. For one thing, it is geriatric: First published in 1918, it underwent its fourth resuscitation in 2000. It is also small and vulnerable—as pokable as the Pillsbury doughboy for determined critics. Its two authors are thoroughly dead, white, and male. And the coddling it enjoys, together with the rules it imposes, makes rebel blood boil—as if Strunk and White were the imperial force in that battle for the language galaxy, the War of Rules versus Usage.

The War began in the late 1950s, pitting liberal language authorities against conservative ones. Taking a stand against elitist notions of correctness, the liberals argued that language derives its validity from actual use, and not from a bunch of prescribed forms. This so-called descriptive approach to standard English was viewed as toxic by the prescriptivists, who not only believed in established rules of expression, but supported a continuum of "worthiness" ranging from illiterate and vernacular to formal.

One such prescriptivist was the essayist and *New Yorker* writer E. B. (Elwyn Brooks) White, who condemned the descriptivist view of language as an "anything goes" position. Encouraged by a publisher, White entered the fray by updating a stern little handbook written in 1919 by William Strunk Jr., his English professor at Cornell—a privately printed book that Strunk had named *The Elements of Style.* White began the new *Elements* with a paean to Strunk and to the professor's belief in "right and wrong." He then livened up Strunk's mundane points regarding grammar and form, closing with a classic piece of advice titled "An Approach to Style," in which he showcased his own skills and warned against the excesses that tempt new and youthful writers. Except in this closing essay, the updated *Elements* addressed mainly a sampling of usage problems and what the authors saw as the most commonly violated fundamentals, a few dozen issues in grammar and composition. A small number of entries supported such fading niceties as the distinctions between *shall* and *will,* or reflected White's antiquated bugaboos—for example, the sin of using *fix* to mean *mend* in formal English.

In White's pre-digital view, there was little use for here-today, deleted-tomorrow language. Good writing was writing that would endure. Language needed vigor, yes, but also a certain hauteur to distinguish it from the rants of the undisciplined. And so he was quick to discourage use of the "offbeat"—vogue words, slang, and advertising-influenced locutions, vigorous though they were. Stick to the standard, White decreed, because "by the time this paragraph sees print, *psyched, nerd, ripoff, dude, geek,* and *funky* will be the words of yesteryear." That was some half century ago—and, dude, those words are still very much around.

But if White missed the mark with a few predictions, he scored a bull's-eye with millions of struggling language users—those seeking a quick, authoritarian fix for shaky writing skills. Selective and quirky as it may be, *The Elements of Style* has succored multitudes of confused students and sloppy communicators. As a guide to the plain English style, the book may yet save America from choking on its own jargon and obfuscations.

What powers the little work as much as anything is its strict formulation of "correctness" in English. This is what sustains Strunk and White's appeal in a world menaced by disorder, and what every writer must take seriously. Most readers quickly sense "correct" or disciplined patterns, whether or not they favor or even understand them. Jarring this sense of correctness can have opposite effects: It can lose readers, jerking them from the subject at hand into concerns about rules and wrongness; or—as *Elements* fails to make clear—if done artfully it can rocket words off the page. It can jolt readers awake. It can set them dancing.

RULES MEANT (SECRETLY) TO BE BENT

Therein lies the whitewash. Both Strunk and White knew well that bending the rules—judiciously breaking them—can give writing its distinction, its edge, its very style. Bending the rules can spring writers from ruts—get them out of themselves, out of the ordinary, and into prose that comes alive, gets noticed, gets published.

As White himself wrote in 1957, "I felt uneasy at posing as an expert on rhetoric, when the truth is I write by ear, always with difficulty and seldom with any exact notion of what is taking place under the hood." And Strunk earlier affirmed that "the best writers sometimes disregard the rules of rhetoric. When they do so, however, the readers will usually find in the sentence some compensating merit, attained at the cost of the violation."

What is "compensating merit?" To me (if I might again violate Style Rule Number One and emerge from the background) it means forceful, stimulating writing. Punchy. Engaging. Several of White's principles—intended to sedate hyperactive students—instead can chill the creative impulse. Try achieving force, originality, or texture without injecting opinion or leaping from the background—without the figures of speech that drive rhetoric; without the breeziness that freshens stale prose; without the foreign borrowings that lend *vivézza;* without the offbeat; without a freaking exclamation point!

Writing is risk taking. We bungee jump from a sentence and pray the cord stops short of catastrophe. We day-trade in language, gambling that a hot image will hold up. White described expression as "a living stream, shifting, changing, receiving new strength from a thousand tributaries." And yet, he advised, "there is simply a better chance of doing well if the writer holds a steady course, enters the stream of English quietly, and does not thrash about."

Who, then, draws strength from these tributaries that feed written expression? Whose prose comes alive in the churning waters? Some writers "thrash about" and go under—but others make waves. White's admonitions may apply to students in a composition class, or to those with riveting stories that best tell themselves. But what happens in today's media-mad din, when becalmed expression meets overloaded and understimulated brains? In White's era, the well-wrought essay found receptive minds; readers willingly entered into quiet dialogue with authors. But the last several decades have brought New Journalism and its rude vitality; in-your-face media; manic Internet blab; the voices of ethnic, pop, youth, and other subcultures; globalization; class meltdown; and mass attention deficit. In this sometimes disparaging, sometimes liberating environment, expressiveness calls for break-a-leg performance. It demands rock-solid command of the language, yes, but also aggressiveness, surprise, exuberance, responsiveness, intensity, *rebelliousness*—most of which White seemed to disdain, except in his own prose.

In his essays and three unconventional children's classics, White went his own way as a writer. Yet in *Elements of Style,* he offered little encouragement for others to do so. Instead, he warned aspiring writers against the "disinclination to submit to discipline." But how inclined to submission was White himself? As a youth, he skimped through Cornell University with "anemic" interests in everything but writing. Shunning his native East Coast, he peddled roach powder in Minneapolis, reported for the Seattle *Times,* and served as a messboy aboard a ship cruising the Aleutian Islands before returning East as an advertising copywriter.

White considered himself disciplined, but took some wild leaps in both his life and his writing—including the death-defying stunt of telling others how to write.

He probably never meant to advise against taking chances, against drawing on all levels of language to animate expression, against demolishing a rule to get attention.

It just comes out that way.

LOCUTIONS WITH SPUNK AND BITE

Perceived correctness can be comforting to the reader, like a tidy house. But what distinguishes a piece of writing is the ambiance—

the environmental mood—that language can create. That's why *locution, locution, locution* is so important to us realtors of words.

In its broad sense, *locution* refers to a particular mode of speech—the use of a word, the turning of a phrase in some stylistic manner. It doesn't have to be fancy. "If a thing can be done, why do it?" was one of poet Gertrude Stein's typical locutions. The British, queenly locution, "We are not amused," is an understated mode of expressing displeasure. And New Yorkers will recognize this locution as one of their own: "That terrific woman, which you should have married her!"

As distinctive ways of saying something, locutions tend to be judged on their aptness, inventiveness, color, sound, rhythm—the qualities that stimulate us, that make expression fetching or thrilling. "Spunk and bite" is our shorthand for such qualities, and in the following chapters we illustrate them with examples both eloquent and funky. My interest—and yours, as a writer in competition with others—lies not with hierarchies of speech, but with a rise from feeble locutions to bell-ringers.

In the bell-ringing category, for example, I would include the jailhouse locutions captured by Tom Wolfe in his novel, *A Man in Full:* "Look, bruvva . . . I ain't tryin' a disrespectchoo . . . I ain't tryin' a sweatchoo, an' I ain't tryin' a play you. So whatchoo doggin' me for?"

Would such locutions have delighted E. B. White? Probably not—but why we be doggin' him about it? Only because few American locutionists stand taller than White, whose animated way with words continues to charm millions. We are not amused, then, to think that his advice to writers concerned itself more with boundaries than White-like flights above the rooftops.

But never mind; for now we are ready to make our own ascent, ready to rise from the slush piles and pedways, ready to soar with E.B. and his like on the wings, the updrafts, of spunk and bite.

SPUNK & BITE

Freshness

THE WALLOP OF THE NEW

TWO

THE PLEASURES OF SURPRISE

Readers love surprise. They love it when a sentence heads one way and jerks another. They love the *boing* of a jack-in-the-box word. They adore images that trot by like a unicorn in pajamas.

Why does surprise please us? Think of it as a survival mechanism: Unexpected stimuli exercise the neurons, keeping brains alert to danger, prey, and available taxis. In fact, a recent study suggests that brains *prefer* surprise to the expected (see the "Synapses of Surprise" sidebar, below).

But enough anthroposemiotic musing! Everyone knows that good writing stimulates readers with inspired, sneaky surprises. It does so at all levels, from surprises based on twists of plot and character to the smaller but keen surprises of language—the ones that concern us here.

Is there a syntax of surprise, a formula for working it into our locutions? Yes and no. Surprise is like one of its vehicles: humor. Try to parse it, and it's hasta la vista, *bubela*. Yet even humor yields an occasional secret to those who won't let it alone. Remember when Woody Allen discovered that "if it bends, it's comedy; if it breaks, it's not"? That's not a bad measure of the unexpected in your prose. Consider these two efforts in a *New York Times* article about the Windows XP operating system. The

SPUNK & BITE

first one breaks apart: "When it comes to obsessive, clean-freak tendencies, Windows XP makes Jack Nicholson in *As Good as It Gets* look like a slob." The image here is labored and arcane—intelligible only to those who have the seen the movie, and even then, too ponderous to allow for surprise. But the second attempt, even with its technical jargon, bends and delivers: "You may have to update its BIOS . . . before installing XP, a procedure about as user-friendly as a wet cat." Bingo! Dry tech-talk, and suddenly I'm smelling damp fur and feeling the scratches.

START WITH THE EXPECTED

Even as you set out to be surprising, gangs of predictable idioms and images will bully their way into first drafts. Let them appear, as they tend to do when the brain is spewing words. But in the editing process, show no mercy. *Occide, verbera, ure!* Kill, beat, and burn—sniff out and destroy everything that smells predictable, clichéd, formulaic, labored, or lazy. Force yourself to fill the gaps with language that hoists a big exclamation point (but not a question mark) above the reader's head.

Use familiar words in a new way; raid the coffers of poetry; recruit fresh words and images from specialized fields; tweak clichés and paired words—not the usual phrase *all agog,* for example, but something surprisingly else *agog (radioactively agog?).* Dare to use unfamiliar words with attention-getting qualities, such as *mofongo* or *barmy.* Concoct your own words now and then, as novelist Jonathan Kellerman did with *firp* (jerk) and *yog* (thug). You won't score surprise every time with these efforts, but you'll create pleasures an editor never expected from the slush mound.

Consider this sentence: *He crosses the consulting room's red carpeting, his grotesquely ugly face like a big toad's.* No surprises here; just a tired word pair (*grotesquely ugly*) and a sorry metaphor. But if you

[11]

were novelist Will Self, author of *How the Dead Live,* you'd have written: "He crosses the consulting room's endometrial carpeting, his marvellously ugly face like a clenched fist in a glove puppet." Three surprises hit me here: "endometrial," because it is shockingly uncarpet-like, yet in keeping with the chapter's context of medical horrors; "marvellously ugly," an effective paradox; and the dead-on "glove puppet" metaphor for a scrunched face.

SYNAPSES OF SURPRISE

Scientists have identified a patch of the forebrain called the *nucleus accumbens* as a center of pleasure in humans. Imaging shows heightened activity in this area of the brain when people receive a reward—whether sugar treats, money, or drugs.

Though researchers have long known monkeys to favor unexpected rewards over expected ones, the same phenomenon has now been identified in humans: Unpredictable stimuli excite the nucleus accumbens, while expected stimuli elicit no response. In the experiment that led to this conclusion, researchers Gregory Burns (Emory University) and E. Read Montague (Baylor College of Medicine) administered squirts of Kool-Aid and plain water to human test subjects in either predictable (alternating) or random patterns. Pleasure-wise, random squirts won it all.

A fresh locution may not be quite the same as Kool-Aid, but writers can extrapolate from the experiment's conclusion: Brains love that little squirt of surprise.

THE BLESSING OF THE PREDICTABLE

Writers may rant about the banality of everyday expression, but they also rely on it. Like every aesthetic element, surprise needs a foil; our habitual speech patterns provide it. A character in a Robert Stone novel remarks, "When you've heard what a Yank has to say in the first five minutes, you've heard everything he'll say the rest of his life." And it's not just Yanks: most everyone communicates in stock patterns using a relatively small working vocabulary. Whatever the topic, people call in the usual skeleton crew of modifiers and images to tackle it, so that everything sounds alike and monotony sweeps the land. When surprise comes along, it's like caffe freddo gushing from the Mojave.

Some writers simply lasso unexpected zingers from their imaginations as the need arises. Others find—or stumble upon—a structure for surprise using one of many rhetorical devices. Here are just a few:

Indirection, beloved by humorists, fakes one way and then reverses for a hook shot: "If love is the answer," says Lily Tomlin, "could you rephrase the question?"

Oxymoron pairs incongruous or contradictory terms to create surprise: engagingly demented; deep inconsequence.

Personification, or **prosopopoeia,** gives life to inanimate or abstract objects: Excuse me, Sir—your liver is on the phone.

Catacosmesis delivers statements in descending order of importance, often ending with a surprising triviality: I ask for peace, prosperity, and a bagel with cream cheese.

Enallage uses one part of speech for another, such as a noun or adjective for a verb: Grammar? I'll grammar you! (See Chapter 16.)

Understatement says surprisingly less about more. For example, a Leslie Stella heroine (Fat Bald Jeff) allows that her hated suitor is "tall and virtually odorless."

Neologisms are invented word formations. Often they build on established word parts, as in schmooseoisie (referring to talk show hosts; "schmooze," with a play on "bourgeoisie") or para-

Freshness / The Wallop of the New

pooch (a dog dropped by parachute). They are good for one surprise each. (See Chapter 14.)

Change of diction from one level of English to another creates surprise if the shift is abrupt and justified. Within just a few lines of a short story ("The Sun, the Moon, the Stars") Junot Díaz shifts from academic diction to street dialect—from a description of European sunbathers as "budget Foucaults" with "massive melanin deficit" to one of Dominican girlfriends who "can't be no more than sixteen" and another of a woman "rocking a dope Ochun-colored bikini." Television scriptwriters, too, speed-shift from one diction to another, as in lines like: "I believe I speak for everyone present here when I say: 'Huh?' " (See Chapter 8.)

Synecdoche and **metonymy** surprise by referring to a part or attribute of something, rather than the thing itself. Noting that he has heard a bearlike sound in the woods, Bill Bryson writes that his pocketknife is "patently inadequate for defending oneself against 400 pounds of *ravenous fur.*" (emphasis mine)

SURPRISE YOURSELF

In the excerpts that follow, I've removed the key words that the authors used to create surprise—or that caught me pleasantly off-guard, at least, when I read them. See if you can equal or better them: try replacing the hint words (in brackets) with something unexpectedly perfect, avoiding the dumbfounding and bizarre. (The actual words used appear in the "Answers" section below.)

1. "At Ozzfest, a pile of bands [played] through their inner children."

2. "His smile beamed everywhere in the large room, as if his teeth were [unbelievably shiny]."

3. "... Martina Hingis, a shrinking star who has become as vulnerable as [a sitting duck]."

4. "He was older than [the hills] now and [likely] to make his century."

5. "Svetlana Ivanova, a 57-year-old pensioner with a mind made up like [something tight-as-a-drum]."

6. "They were foragers and gatherers, can redeemers, the people who [swayed] through subway cars with paper cups."

7. "How much cooler it is to save the world from the Nazis than [fret] over the NASDAQ."

8. "Sister Grace believed the proof of God's creativity [came] from the fact that you could not surmise the life, even remotely, of his humblest shut-ins."

9. "If there are a number of visually interesting ways to shoot two heads floating in an endless expanse of H$_2$O, Kentis has succeeded in finding [not too many] of them."

ANSWERS

1. trolled (Ben Ratliff, *The New York Times*); 2. strangely iridescent (Jane Smiley, *Moo*); 3. dunk-tank victim (Selena Roberts, *The New York Times*); 4. kerosene, strong (Annie E. Proulx, "The Bunchgrass Edge of the World"); 5. marine's bed (Michael Wines, *The New York Times*); 6. yawed (Don DeLillo, *Underworld*); 7. swivet (Maureen Dowd, *The New York Times*); 8. eddied (Don DeLillo, *Underworld*); 9. exactly none (Mike D'Angelo, *Esquire*).

SURPRISINGLY APT

Ultimately, the devices of surprise may set up the pins, but they don't guarantee the strike. The essence of surprise is in its timing and execution: fast, graceful, and apt. Aptness is paramount. The best surprise of all may be how precisely an unexpected word or image pops a message. Unexpected is easy; unexpectedly perfect helps separate writers from hacks.

[15]

Freshness / The Wallop of the New

THREE

EXTREME EXPRESSION

Try describing the extraordinary—say, the extremely large—and see what happens. Immediately the verbal channels are swamped by used-up modifiers: *great; huge; enormous*—all yesterday's news. *Cosmic.* What isn't? *Way cosmic.* Way lame. Most writers wish to go beyond such adjectives, to boldly go where no word maven has gone before. But a rolling blackout darkens the brain. Life in the universe seems beyond the wattage of language. The events of one day drain the thesaurus. So many extraordinary things, so few terms to describe them.

Reaching for extremes, nonwriters (or lazy writers) fall back on the vocabulary of disbelief: "It was just . . . *incredible.* I mean, *unbelievable.* Absolutely *mind-boggling.*" Such terms may define the borders of one's credulity; unfortunately, they fail to distinguish the Piazza San Marco from a piece a'pizza.

Extraordinary subjects call for the might of imagery—power imagery, delivered as extreme figures of speech. I've dubbed such figures *megaphors*—and, for descriptions of the extremely small, *miniphors.* These special breeds of metaphor, simile, and hyperbole go the distance to catch the reader's imagination.

KILLER MEGAPHORS

A megaphor uses images of imposing size, force, or notoriety to augment a subject in an attention-getting way. Make it novel and clever and it's doubly hot—as hot as these megaphors were in their day: *killer abs; avalanche selling; Dow Jones meltdown; smashmouth football.*

Fresh is best, but used imagery often can be retrofitted for new applications: *industrial-strength attitude; slam-dunk dissertation; poster child for failed diets.* In dissenting from a majority opinion of the Supreme Court, Justice Ruth Bader Ginsburg once called the majority's rationale "nothing short of a titanic surrender to the implausible." As an image, the *Titanic* may be rusted out, but Ginsburg salvaged it with steel-plated moxie.

Megaphors have thundered throughout world literature, augmenting everything from mead hall beasts to gumshoe hangovers. Dante summoned the great towers of Montereggione as megaphors for the titans of Hell. Whitman raised his "barbaric yawp" to celebrate himself. Joyce's Daedalus went forth to "forge in the smithy of my soul the uncreated conscience of my race." Chicago, now gentrified and stockyard-free, lives forever as the "Hog Butcher for the World . . . City of the Big Shoulders" in the megaphors of Carl Sandburg.

Our frenetic culture has every type of writer scrambling for extreme expression. Journalists and writers of ads, scripts, and speeches live by images that outdistance, one-up, or out-hype all previous takes on a subject. As *New York Times* staffer Ira Berkow noted, "Incredible may be an understatement in a sports world of galloping hyperbole." Hyperbole rules in all spheres of communication, including politics. Did a *black hole* in foreign policy give

Freshness / The Wallop of the New

rise to *the mother of all insurgencies?* Is party principle *melting faster than the polar ice caps?*

MIGHTY MAMMA NATURE

For your own extreme imagery, you can start with natural forces: *She's a Mount St. Helens waiting to erupt. There's an ozone hole in his thinking. Like El Niño hitting on La Niña.* But when such cataclysmic megaphors as earthquakes and tidal waves wear thin (even in love scenes), writers need other forces to power their images. One such force is the high-profile personality, real or fictional. A sports agent is called the "Moses" of his clients. The old Jerry Seinfeld character cries, "She's like a beautiful Godzilla!" Names such as Florence Nightingale and Martin Luther King connote big virtues, while such Evil Empire denizens as Hitler and Lord Voldemort ratchet up the villainy. And by combining columns A and B, one creates fearsome hybrids: *Watch out—she's Mother Theresa meets Hannibal Lecter!*

While they're hot, superstars and other news makers can muscle up a sentence. When *Buffy the Vampire Slayer* ruled prime time, a phrase like *Buffy Summers unleashed* would have shattered walls. But megaphorists must weigh the shelf life of ephemeral imagery. In the first paragraph of this chapter, I risked an allusion to California's rolling blackouts—now ancient history. A safer reference might have been to China's Three Gorges Dam, the ongoing construction of which reporters have called "planetary in scale." I shoulda said, "our brain hits the Three Gorges Dam."

And don't forget: Arcane megaphors may delight a savvy audience, but their immensity will be lost on the unknowing. Novelist Martin Amis writes of a "Mahabharata of pain"; but to appreciate the image, a reader must be hip to the *Mahabharata—*

[18]

a Hindu epic of some hundred thousand couplets. To use or not to use? One takes stock of one's audience, and gives it one's best.

THE INCREDIBLE SHRINKING MINIPHOR

The wee components of the universe challenge writers to venture ever shrimpier in their metaphors, finding new ways to downsize the extremely small and insignificant. Conventional modifiers—*tiny, diminutive, microscopic*—cause less shrinkage than a cold-wash cycle. *Roget's'* downsizings offer a few more choices: *skosh,* from the Japanese *sukoshi,* means "a little bit"; *minikin* refers to a petite and dainty person; *soupçon* means "just a suspicion of a trace"; and *scintilla* is a hissy word for "a piddling amount."

But a thesaurus can plunge only so far into the infinitesimal. Enter miniphors: metaphorical figures for the extraordinarily puny. One thinks first of the smallest entities, subatomic particles. Though short on sensuality, they speak of diminishing space and have wonderfully loopy names: "quark," "lepton," "gluon," "muon," and so on. *A paycheck the size of a muon* is something most writers can relate to. Other miniphors can be pulled from numerical imagery; for example, *nano-spans of attention,* meaning "billionths of a span." Even further down the minus powers of ten, *picos, femtos,* and *zeptos* make *nanos* look gargantuan.

Sometimes the best miniphors, however, are based on moderately small items that the average reader can imagine. To physicists, particles in cloud chambers may connote "dinky"; but the smallness of zits, peanuts, and mustard seeds can be better pictured and felt by others. Likewise, a *gnat's-breath attention span* seems as brief as a nano-span—even briefer if I imagine an out-of-shape gnat. And I could say, arcanely, that someone's authority extends about one *Planck length*—a reference to the smallest reducible interval of time and space. But *parsley on the fish,* as one executive described her board's role, says it even smaller.

IMAGERY, BIG AND SMALL

Highway tragedies, toiletries—anything in the universe is grist for the creation of boffo metaphors. Here's a sampling of what writers have appropriated lately to augment or diminish a subject. To build your own stock of extreme images, keep an eye out for the next big or little thing that has yet to be sucked into metaphor.

"...a fatal freeway pileup of random metaphors, a grisly shooting spree of meaningless analogies." [on the prose style of Sarah, Duchess of York] (—Mark Steyn, *Wall Street Journal*)

"Steinbrenner has littered the Major Deegan with the road kill of managers past." (—Claire Smith, *The New York Times*)

"[H]is thoughts churned like ... the sea lung: a heavy sludge of ice under fog." (—E. Annie Proulx, *The Shipping News*)

"It was Arnaud Clément again, the [tennis player]...who stands the size of hotel soap." (—Selena Roberts, *The New York Times*)

"Prince Charles referred to it [London's Millennium Dome] as a 'monstrous blanc-mange'." (—Michael Specter, *The New Yorker*)

"[John Daly's] backswing is longer than Tolstoy." (—Rick Reilly, *Who's Your Caddy?*)

"[The film *Fahrenheit 9/11*] is employed to pump air into one of the great sagging blimps of our sorry, mediocre, celeb-rotten culture." (—Christopher Hitchens, *Slate*)

"[H]e circles the globe like a ship carrying nuclear waste." (—Salman Rushdie, *The Ground Beneath Her Feet*)

"[T]he author manages to deploy all the standard missiles of postmodernism." (—Will Blythe, *Esquire*)

"The universe poured down in a bombing onslaught of heavenly vomit." (—Jonathan Safran Foer, *Everything Is Illuminated*)

"Opponents [in boxing] are not merely defeated as in a game, but are 'decked', 'stiffed', 'starched', 'iced', . . . 'annihilated'. " (—Joyce Carol Oates, *On Boxing*)

OTHER FIXES

Writing is about force, about driving home an idea. And extreme imagery is one good means to that end—but only one. For reducing or enlarging a subject, there are other devices—among them the affixes (attachments to words) that mean "greater" or "lesser" in a figurative way.

Consider, for example, the diminishing suffixes used in the following sentence: *Fact*oids *from source*lings *get little respect in serious writing; fiction editors look for characters, not character*ettes; *for thoughts, not thought*sies.

Augmenting devices include such prefixes as *hyper-* and *ultra-*, though these can become as tiresome as a locution I overheard in a Florida dockside restaurant: "See that white boat? That's a *multi-, multi-, multi-, multi-million-dollar* boat."

Understatement, which frees readers to blow a hint out of all proportion, is another powerful augmenter. *"Oh, it's nothing," said Mom.* (Better call an ambulance.)

And even a miniphor can indicate great force or size when used in a contrasting analogy. Describing a river gorge in Montana, Peter Martin wrote in *Esquire*: "The sick waterflow here (which

[21]

Freshness / The Wallop of the New

makes the Grand Canyon look like Thomas Kinkade's backyard stream) creates huge standing waves."

From sweetly painted rills to stretch Hummers, the world keeps churning out new phenomena—personalities, deeds, follies, scandals, harms, calamities, physical frontiers—to be referenced in extreme metaphors, brooking no return to those whimpers of disbelief. Novelist William Gass once said, "I love metaphor the way some people love junk food." So the next time you're describing the extraordinary, why not reach for a Whopper?

SPUNK & BITE

FOUR

WRITERS' WORDS, DROP BY DOTTLE

As every writer comes to learn, producing a crop after crop of *oeuvres* exhausts the loam of expression. Words become sapped by overuse. Sentences, descriptive passages, and lines of poetry go limp. Creative roots cry for infusion.

Have I told you the parable of my potted grapefruit? The plant, which I proudly grew from seed, flourished until the day its foliage sulked, drooped, and entered a state of lassitude. Drenchings and fresh soil prompted only deathbed twitches. Finally, abandoning delusions of having a gardener's thumb, I brought home a sea-blue slosh of nutrients to be administered drop-by-drop—a mere seven drops with each watering. And, lo, within a day the leaf blades snapped to. Jessant shoots erupted like virescent starbursts. An attar of citrus spiced the air, and perfumes it even now. And so might it be with those who write—those who would invigorate vocabularies gone creachy: Vitalization by the drop.

Many a writer has resolved to master the dictionary A to Z, or bulk up the brain with vocabulary-building tomes. But such enterprises tend to fizzle, which for readers may not be a bad thing; an inundation of new words can create a garden of monstrous locutions. Eyedropper enrichment—say, at the rate of about seven

[23]

Freshness / The Wallop of the New

new words a week—allows one to savor and test each word, to integrate it into one's style before sounding like Buckley-meets-Pynchon on Miracle-Gro.

WRITERS' WORDS

The planet groans with word resources, many of them aimed at language hobbyists, or *logophiles*. In his *Dictionary of Misunderstood, Misused & Mispronounced Words,* lexicographer Laurence Urdang wisecracks—and who could disagree?—that an "enchiridion of arcane and recondite sesquipedalian items will appeal to the oniomania of an eximious Gemeinschaft." Translation: Certain exceptional types like to buy collections of big, unusual words.

Writers appreciate recondite words as much as the next language junkie, but they don't want readers gagging on them. After all, an asphyxiating vocabulary flirts with what novelist Jonathan Franzen calls the "status model" of authorship, in which the *artiste* disdains popularity and holds that "difficulty tends to signal excellence." In Franzen's opposing "contract model," a novelist promises to *connect* with readers in exchange for their investment of time and attention and to be accountable should any reader "crack a tooth on a hard word." ("Mr. Difficult," *The New Yorker*)

Those who want to connect, then, stock their journals with *writers'* words—not always the plainest or best-known words, but those somehow rewarding to the reader. Franzen himself uses words such as *solipsistic* (self-absorbed) and *pemmican* (a kind of meat loaf) in his argument, but they turn out to be pretty good chaws in context.

For special purposes, a writers' word can be anything from *firkin* to *floccinaucinihilipilification*. But to earn a place in an author's working vocabulary, a word should be at least one of the following:

- Precise: *tor* (hilltop rock heap)
- Concise: *mulct* (defraud, as of money)
- Euphonious: *fanfaronade* (bluster)
- Onomatopoetic: *williwaw* (violent squall)
- Forceful: *fulgent* (dazzlingly bright)
- Evocative: *mojo* (charmed object)
- Fun: *cachinnate* (laugh immoderately)
- Fresh: *nimiety* (an abundance instead of, say, stale *plethora*)

What if a word is likely to be outside the reader's active or half-known vocabulary? Then even undefined, it should lend some special aura, some majesty or exoticism, to the context. Perhaps the unknown word reveals itself by sound or placement—*steam purled* (flowed in curls) *up from the pavement*—or begs to be looked up, like *scumble* (to soften brilliant color). In my grapefruit parable, I planted what seemed to be three such words: *jessant* (shooting upward), *virescent* (tending toward green), and *attar* (a perfume obtained from flowers). Did they add a certain flavor, or merely squirt in your eye?

FINDING FRESH DROPS

Where does one find writers' words not yet squeezed to death? Self-help compilations such as the *Word Smart* series (Princeton Review) can provide a few, but such big lists—many of them geared toward readers preparing for SAT tests—can be daunting. And although word-a-day desk calendars deliver a manageable dosage, the few winners among their 365 offerings often get lost as desks pile up and days fly by. Instead, I favor collections that include droll, well-informed discourse to slow things down; for example, *Word Watch* (Holt), which features Anne H. Soukhanov's riffs on emerging words such as *mamou* (something big and important). Another recent favorite is *The Oxford American Writer's Thesaurus,* rich in word commentary by silver-tongued authors. New resources keep appearing on word-and-language shelves; one simply has to browse the shelves to see just which slosh of nutrients will perk up the old vocabulary.

Some writers like to go looking for words in all the wrong (but of course right) places: pop-culture media, technical handbooks and glossaries, collections of malediction. Compilations of obscure and antiquated words, including old slang dictionaries, house quaint or cocky "foundlings"—forgotten terms ready to *trampoose* through modern contexts. And with Internet sites like the Rap Dictionary, *www.rapdict.org,* y'all gon be *glemmin'* (shining up) ya sentences wit dope words, yo.

The freshest items, however, are most likely to surface in the world's active flow of expression—literary, journalistic, ethnic, and subcultural. Prize specimens swim by regularly. And if Sunday pundits and other word mavens seize a few of them, so what? Individual writers with keen eyes, notebooks, and the patience to look up words will still net their share. Anyone is free to snatch isolated words from what they read and hear. Outside of trademarked names, no one owns a word—not even poets associated with, say, *darkling* or *diverged.*

My recent pickings from literature include *flense* (to skin a whale, or figuratively, to flay) from Michael Chabon; *peridot* (green, transparent gemstone) from Sandra McPherson; and *camorra* (secret society) from Anne Fadiman. I'll keep them handy for some inspired use.

INTERNET WORD-A-DAY SOURCES: A SAMPLING

Vocabulary sort of *spavined* (broken down)? You can find revitalizing words each day on sites likes these, some of which (as of this writing) will send word features to your E-mail by free subscription. Sample words (in italics) are from the referenced sites; I've shortened the definitions.

THE WORD SPY [*www.wordspy.com*]. Paul McFedries' sharp-eyed collection of recent coinages. Includes context, background, sightings, and quotes. Indexed archives.
   Invacuate: to hold people in a building for safety.

A DEFINITION A DAY [*vocabula.com*]. From The Vocabula Review. Selects words with "an aura of fun or majesty." Stellar columns, quizzes, and random words.
   Weanling: a newly weaned child or animal.

WORD OF THE DAY FROM LEXICO PUBLISHING [*dictionary.reference.com/wordoftheday*]. Well organized; includes archives and quotes. Free E-mail delivery.
   Wayworn: travel-weary.

WORTHLESS WORD FOR THE DAY [*home.mn.rr.com/wwftd*]. Anything but worthless. Features "obscure, abstruse, and/or recondite words" that are often writers' words. Archive. Free E-mail delivery.
   Muzzy: muddled, confused.

A.WORD.A.DAY [*wordsmith.org/awad*]. [See description elsewhere in this chapter.] Free E-mail delivery.
   Hobbledehoy: an awkward young fellow.

MERRIAM-WEBSTER'S WORD OF THE DAY [*www.m-w.com*]. Solid, informative. Features etymology and usage examples. Archive. Free E-mail delivery.
   Quidnunc: a busybody.

[27]

Freshness / The Wallop of the New

WEB OF WORDS

Perhaps the most dynamic—if messy—word source these days is the Internet, where some sites offer useful vocabulary in delayed-release doses (see sidebar, "Internet Word-a-Day Sources: A Sampling") and others overwhelm the frontal lobes with Scrabble-babble, bloggerese, and link madness.

Of the sites offering daily infusions of new words, the most renowned is A.Word.A.Day (*www.wordsmith.org/awad*). Bubbling with features and claiming some half million devotees, it has generated a best-selling book from its word archives (Aru Garg's *A Word A Day,* published by Wiley) and a follow-up collection. At no cost, subscribers receive a daily selected word and commentary by E-mail.

In most word-a-day services, many selections will be technical, silly, arcane, or ordinary (though often with eccentric histories). One service taught me the word *dottle,* which refers to the bit of charred pipe tobacco remaining in a pipe bowl. The source calls all its terms "worthless," but one never knows when so genial a word might animate a metaphor—or even a chapter title.

Realistically, only a few of the daily words received each month from Internet sources will be writers' words; but here's the point: You will see them, and see them at a reasonable pace for vocabulary-building. When eager for more, you can dive into the sites' archives of prior words and swim among the *momes* (boors) and *bonces* (heads). Should you need to see the words in other contexts, additional usages can usually be found through search engines like Google.

But once again, the big-mamou question: Should you use a word you fear will stump your readers? Absolutely—if you adore it, haven't used too many puzzlers elsewhere, and believe it to be what Mark Twain would call the "intensely right word." After all, what sweeter lagniappe for readers than a new *mot juste* for their delectation?

Freshness / The Wallop of the New

FIVE

UPGRADING YOUR COLORS

Maybe it has to do with the blue and yellow rings in the crib, or the red walls we painted in our student apartments. But for both writer and reader, color is memory, color is mood, color is meaning. With color, we can strike the mind's eye dead center.

The trouble is, most color imagery consists of worn metaphors: *as blue as the sky; as red as a ruby.* These colors have lost their charge. You can call a sky "steel-gray" or "ashen," but such clichés will not distinguish the feeling of a particular sky from that of all other gray skies. When you want the power of precision, you must stop and fashion your own hues. In his novel *Yellow Dog,* Martin Amis created just the shade of gray he wanted, writing that "[the] motorway was a seething, sizzling mess of drenched metal and rubber, under skies the colour of dog's lips."

Color need be no more than a brushstroke to evoke a mood— unless you happen to be Vincent van Gogh. With Vincent's feel for color, concision could go the way of his earlobe, as in this letter to his brother:

> The sky . . . not white, but a lilac which can hardly be deciphered, white shimmering with red, blue, and yellow in which

everything is reflected, and which one feels everywhere above one, which is vaporous and merges into the mist below—harmonizing everything in a gamut of delicate gray.

(Drenthe, Netherlands, 1883)

Vincents we are not, and modern audiences won't sit still for fifty-word rhapsodies. But color is ours—ours to use in ways that capture experiences and stir readers.

With all the associations it triggers, one color can be worth a yard of paragraphs. Writers create special colors for special meanings, but sometimes even a basic hue can speak buckets: *purple house, red fur, blue teeth.* In fact, Alexander Theroux finds blue, red, and yellow worth 268 charming pages in his *Primary Colors,* a compendium of color occurrences in myth, science, literature, and so on—required browsing for any serious colorist, along with *Secondary Colors,* a 312-page companion volume about orange, purple, and green.

But sometimes standard colors are off-target. Sometimes you want readers not only to see an exact shade, but to enter it. You want to create an aura, reveal a point of view. When John Updike describes a street of "old asphalt sidings the tint of bruise and dung," he underscores the sad ambience of *Rabbit at Rest.*

Clichéd metaphors like *green as grass* or *emerald green* not only look lazy, but are too exhausted to flash color across a page. "We need to boost our range of greens," said Diane Ackerman in *A Natural History of the Senses,* "to describe the almost squash-yellow green of late winter grass, the achingly fluorescent green of the leaves of high summer." And a little surprise and whimsy in the spectrum might not hurt: In *Harry Potter and the Chamber of Secrets,* J. K. Rowling boosted the range of eye colors with the line, "His eyes are as green as a fresh pickled toad."

[31]

Freshness / The Wallop of the New

A LITERARY PAINT SET

Writers have long created imaginative hues to describe their worlds. Although "new" colors fade quickly in literature, literary minds can generate more tints than a shelf of graphic software. Here's a ten-color starter set for inspiration.

Red. "...blood the color of autumn dahlias bubbling from the nose and mouth."

(—Sandra Cisneros)

Pink. "...a face pink like St. Nicholas."

(—Ralph Ellison)

Gray. "T-shirts of...narcolepsy gray..."

(—Gary Shteyngart)

Brown. "...a counter spread with hams as brown as violins."

(—Alain De Botton)

Turquoise. "...[a foster parents' house] the color of a tropical lagoon on a postcard thirty years out of date, a Gauguin syphilitic nightmare."

(—Janet Fitch)

Red-brown. "...[A] mustache...the color of a turned slice of apple."

(—Michael Chabon)

Yellow-brown. "The Downs are yellow-brown, like the flanks of lions."

(—Helen Dunmore)

Yellow. "...one bird or two—and they were the yellow of all yellows, the kind of yellow that every other yellow secretly wishes to be."

(—Redmond O'Hanlon)

Orange. ". . . an orange dress the color of a mussel's lip."

(—Jim Harrison)

Blonde. "My hair is the color of chopped maples."

(—Carolyn Forché)

EXPAND YOUR PALETTE

How do some of the best writers upgrade their Crayolas? The following techniques show up in their lovely scribblings:

Fresh visual metaphors.
Striking out clichés like *lobster-red* is easy enough; the challenge is to find brand-new visual imagery that also fits the style and tone of a piece. Landscapes must be scoured for offbeat but recognizable objects to denote particular colors—and perhaps something more.

Almost any setting, however prosaic, yields unusual or symbolic items. Waiting in a dentist's chair? Note the color of the chair's upholstery, the mouth rinse, hygienic masks, plaster gums, anything familiar. Later, you may find yourself describing a bedroom "repainted a dentist's-office mauve," as Gary Shteyngart does in *The Russian Debutante's Handbook,* or a rainy day the color of dental X-rays.

Color imagery should be fresh and inventive, but not constantly over-the-top. A "man with skin the color of boiled newspaper" pushes the envelope, but Michael Chabon got away with it in *The Amazing Adventures of Kavalier & Clay,* his sometimes-farcical novel of the 1940s comic book world. Here, images of a building "the color of a stained shirt collar," or of somebody's

[33]

"lung-colored socks," have the feel of Sunday funnies. But in less-comical moods Chabon scales back, describing "skin the color of almond hulls" and "a sunrise the color of bourbon and ash."

The sky makes for a good practice canvas. Every mood suggests a different swatch, whether "ash-bourbon" (Chabon), "indecipherable-lilac" (van Gogh), or "like the pink tongue of a thirsty dog" (Isaac Babel, *Odessa*). But too much image can bring on the clouds. It's hard to picture a sky "as blue as the ribbon on a prize-winning lamb," as Chabon describes it. The blasted lamb keeps getting in the way.

Sandra Cisneros, imagist supreme, colors the world of her novel *Caramelo* through the sensibilities of its Mexican and Mexican-American characters. A church isn't beige, but "the color of *flan*"; a washerwoman is a "fried-*tortilla* color"; Mexican shawls are "as black as Coyotepec pottery, as black as *huitlacoche,* the corn mushroom, as true-black as an *olla* of fresh-cooked black beans"; a door has yellowed to "the color of Mexican sour cream." Even if some readers miss the precise shade, they'll still get the flavor and texture.

Inventive abstract metaphors.

In *The Adventures and Misadventures of Maqroll,* Álvaro Mutis writes of a ship's dirty white surface as having "[a] coat of grime . . . the color of misery, of irreparable decadence, of desperate, incessant use." As color consultants will chirp, every hue suggests certain abstract qualities. In literature it works the other way, too: abstractions evoke colors. (Happiness registers blue, right?) Writers can avoid color clichés not only with fresh concrete imagery, but with well-wrought abstractions. What color is an airport baggage claim area on a bad day? For Jonathan Franzen in *The Corrections,* not gray, not yellowish, but "the color of car-sickness."

[34]

Adjectives with personality.
Colors can be anthropomorphized—animated with adjectives usually applied to people. But overused pairings like *angry red* won't knock anyone out—better to go with *ballistic red* or *berserk red*. In *About This Life,* Essayist Barry Lopez unleashes a rainbow of behavioral tints to describe fired anagama pottery: "[H]ere . . . are raucous purples, coy yellows, prosaic blues, belligerent reds, and what . . . poet Denise Levertov called ardent whites."

Technical names.
For the color cognoscenti, pigment-based technical names like "cerulean blue," "Naples yellow," and "alizarin red" conjure a specific image—no further modification necessary. But for general audiences, such specialized names serve less to delineate than to create lyrical effects. A poem in a literary journal might thus use the terms *solferino* (purplish-pink) or *vitelline* (egg-yolk yellow), precisely for their esoteric feel.

Thesaurus and word-menu lists.
Though most color terms provided by such resources are worn or arcane, some will serve nicely for workaday assignments. *Roget's,* for example, reminds us of *tawny, saffron, ochre,* and *jaundiced* yellows, and *Word Menu* recalls such reds as claret, rose madder, and garnet.

Designer nomenclature.
Writers can take a few cues, if not specific nomenclature, from the companies and designers who create names for product colors— names such as Winestone Pearl, Sandstone Metallic, Dusty Olive, Oatmeal Heather, Putty, and Peacock. The commercial color "Stonewashed Indigo" resonates for a jeans-buying audience, just

[35]

as the phrase "washed duns" does for readers of a Barry Lopez essay about the Mojave Desert.

Armed with an extended palette, the writer must now exercise the usual skills of strategic deployment and restraint. Resist such redundancies as "*bright* fire-engine red" and "*blue-gray* Wedgewood." Still, as you set out to paint with words, consider fearlessly the century-old epithet in Nathalia Crane's *The Vestal:* "Every gaudy color / Is a bit of truth."

JOLTINGLY FRESH ADVERBS

"He cumbrously consulted a file he withdrew from a briefcase of achingly sensible utility," wrote novelist Will Self in *How the Dead Live.*

Cumbrously. Achingly. Amazing what a smart *-ly* will do. These attention-getting modifiers represent a new and fashionable version of an old friend: the adverb.

Adverbs, you might have learned before nodding off in class, are the things that modify whatever adjectives do not. Adjectives modify nouns and pronouns, as in "I released the *emergency* brake, *silly* me." Adverbs put a spin on everything else—verbs, adjectives, other adverbs: "I *half intentionally* released the emergency brake, *suicidally* silly me."

In Composition 101, the adverb came with certain interdictions: Don't prop up every verb with adverbs. (Not *ran speedily,* but *raced* or *dashed.*) Avoid adverbs in dialogue tags. (Not *cried loudly,* but *howled* or *wailed.*) Delete redundant adverbs, as in *glitters brightly.*

Blame such strictures if you remember the adverb as some kind of prosthetic device. But the truth is that certain adverbial forms are among the hottest locutions in contemporary prose.

[37]

THE TELLTALE ADVERB

We rely on adverbs to reveal all sorts of information about the things they modify. They tell us where, when, how, how much, and so on. Did your manuscript arrive *early, late,* or *never?* That's worth knowing, as is the sense of the arrival: *"ridiculously* early," says an adjective-like adverb.

Most adverbs are formed by the addition of *-ly* to an adjective—e.g., *lavish* becomes *lavishly.* And wherever English is lavishly nuanced, writers have been working this adverbial form into smart locutions. Here's the method: Take a forceful adjective (say, *withering*), add *-ly* to make it an adverb, combine it with the target word (say, *cute*), and *voilà—witheringly cute,* a burst of wry wit, a ministatement.

Critic Michiko Kakutani of *The New York Times* has been lavish in her use of *-ly* adverbs, as have many of her colleagues at the newspaper. Some time ago she described a British novelist's prose as "engagingly demented." Legions of *-ly* locutions have followed over the years, including "casually authoritative" and "eye-crossingly voluminous." Meanwhile, her colleagues have come up with "beguilingly Boswellian" (Joseph J. Ellis), "laughably archival" (Dinitia Smith), "jesuitically contradictory" (Bruce Grierson), and "genetically goofy" (David Carr).

Arts reviewers (and blurbists) everywhere seem enamored of the device, and little wonder; it offers an alternative to shopworn critical adjectives like *brilliant, gripping,* or *plodding.* It can also tweak such adjectives toward fresh meanings, as in *yawningly brilliant.*

MANNER AND DEGREE

These examples feature what grammarians call "adverbs of manner." They reveal the way in which a thing or quality is distinguished. According to yet another *New York Times* critic, Allesandra Stanley, a new television show was "deliciously horrifying," distinguishing it from other modes of horrifyingness. Writers also toy with so-called adverbs of degree, which answer the question "how much"? Performances are routinely described as "hugely boring" or "minutely entertaining."

When a term and its modifier seem paradoxical, like *horrifying* and *deliciously,* they form the rhetorical device known as the oxymoron. Oxymorons can produce any number of effects: sarcasm, incisiveness, archness (i.e., roguishness, sauciness). But not all adverbial zingers employ the incongruity of terms in contrast. Many reach for metaphor, as in *lashingly funny,* or hyperbole (exaggeration), as in *woundingly beautiful.* In addition, critics often find *-ly* forms suited to the put-down. *Slate*'s Gary Lutz called the grammar chapter of the fifteenth edition of *The Chicago Manual of Style* "perversely unhelpful"—though I deviantly disagree.

For an especially mannered tone, some writers pile up the syllables, as in "hilariously epigrammatic," Nancy Franklin's way of describing a campy sitcom character for *The New Yorker.*

AWFULLY DECENT OF YOU, JEEVES

No one is sure when and where the *-ly* adverb acquired such mannered traits, but nineteenth- or twentieth-century England is a fair bet. One can visualize the ivory cigarette holders, the stiff upper lips, the *awfully*s and *terribly*s drawled with ironic intent.

[39]

"So *frightfully* rich," remarked Lady Redesdale, Diana Mitford's mother, in 1928 of her son-in-law-to-be. The *-ly* adverb of manner remains as British as actor Stephen Fry, who in the film *Cold Comfort Farm* blubbers to his heartthrob: "I'm *engorgingly* in love with you!"

Evolving from the suffix *-lich,* which meant "like," the *-ly* adverbial ending has been around for centuries in English. Some six hundred years before the Schweppes tonic "Ambassador" launched the advertising catchphrase "curiously refreshing," Chaucer was there with "curiously arrayed." Adverbs modifying adjectives, as in "*curiously* dainty things," show up as early as 1570.

In the American idiom, national figures ranging from Richard Nixon to Microsoft's Bill Gates have helped propagate this mannered locution. Nixon's "perfectly clear" was echoed in countless imitations. And when Gates described his products as "insanely great," he pushed an overused adjective about as far as it can go by using an adverb of degree. Not that America's youth culture, with its *totally*s, *incredibly*s and *amazingly*s, needs any nudge toward adverbs of manner and degree—but some fresh ones wouldn't be so bad.

MATCH THE *-LY* ADVERBS WITH THEIR MATES

What makes a winning *-ly* locution? It might be a paradoxical or farcical relationship between the adverb and what it modifies; it might be a strikingly apt relationship. Novelty, rhythm, and sound also weigh in. See if these virtues help you match the adverbs on the left with the verbs, adjectives, and adverbs on the right. (The phrases in parentheses indicate the subjects of these *-ly* locutions when they originally appeared in print).

SPUNK & BITE

1. dormantly	a. ordinary (plot structure)
2. gloriously	b. fervent (devotion)
3. scarily	c. naive (conviction)
4. militantly	d. Mormon (guy from Philly)
5. incongruously	e. hostile (speech)
6. juicily	f. unclever (writer)
7. resolutely	g. ridiculous (role as pirate)
8. wittily	h. intricate (dance step)
9. inflammatorily	i. prosaic (men's fashions)
10. metaphysically	j. uproarious (doings)

ANSWERS:

1. d (Patricia Marx, *The New Yorker*); 2. j (*Kirkus Reviews*); 3. b (Sarah Miller, *The New York Times Book Review*); 4. i (Judith Thurman, *The New Yorker*); 5. a (Janet Maslin, *The New York Times*); 6. g (David Denby, *The New Yorker*); 7. f (Bruno Maddox, *The New York Times Book Review*); 8. h (Richard Eder, *The New York Times*); 9. e (John Updike, *The New Yorker*); 10. c (Lydia Davis, *Granta*).

FARCICALLY ADVANCED

The adverbial form got a big, if farcical, boost when satirists Henry Beard and Chris Cerf gave it a name in their *Official Politically Correct Dictionary and Handbook* (1992). Calling it the "adverbially premodified adjectival lexical unit," they defined it as

[41]

the most frequently used linguistic form in the construction of culturally appropriate language. "Physically inconvenienced," "involuntarily leisured" . . . are examples.

Perhaps those who are "follicularly challenged," such as this writer, are partial to the form. But at any rate, quirky adverbs tend to make the most striking -*ly* locutions, whether used in farce, feature writing, or even the occasional work of literature. Common adverbs such as *wonderfully* and *fantastically* have lost their original force. Along with *terrifically, genuinely,* and *actually,* such adverbs moil to intensify bland words like *nice* and *good,* only to subsume them in a hum of white noise.

Exhausted adverbs cannot intensify weary adjectives. Recent attempts seen in book reviews result in such babble as "genuinely invaluable," "deeply pleasurable," and "thoroughly readable." Such adverbs work better when, instead of trying to prop up words, they jerk the rug out from under them: *profoundly vapid,* or "delightfully tacky" (the Hooters restaurant slogan)—that sort of thing. But even these constructions are facile oxymorons, and soon they join the heap of clichés. Locutions that work too hard can grow as tiresome as facile ones. Again in desperation, reviewers stock such phrases as "thunderingly banal" and "bracingly ironic" in their lexicons—becoming, in the locution of one movie critic, "poundingly predictable."

Other writers forge -*ly* locutions that are good for one use only, as a quick way to delineate something or deliver information. In *Esquire,* for example, Will Blythe described a novelist who burned himself out on drugs as having died "in 1978 as a gloriously used-up forty-eight-year-old speed freak." And with that, Blythe's slick locution was "used up"—not gloriously, not outrageously, but aptly so.

[42]

Texture

WRITING INTO THE MOOD

SEVEN

TENSE: A STICKY CHOICE

The raft sinks. He clings to her. She shoves him away.
The raft sank. He clung to her. She shoved him away.

Every narrative has a base tense, the one that moves the action forward. Which one is best for your story—past or present? It's like choosing between potential spouses: Past is well established, admired for its self-control and sense of perspective; Present is a relative upstart, not universally liked—but with an in-the-moment quality that can be thrillingly edgy.

In the short run—say, for chapter drafts or short stories—you could flirt with each and see how it works out. For a love saga or memoir, Past's amplitude of time might win your heart. For a thriller, Present's nervous uncertainty might be endearing. Brief commitment is involved here, but no sacred vows.

For book-length projects, however, choosing a base tense is akin to walking down the aisle. In the long course of your writing, your choice of tense will affect every page. It will lock in a mood that may or may not be right for the story; it will steer editors' reactions and resonate among reviewers and readers.

Which shall it be as you launch sentence one? Sylvia Plath might have chosen "It is a queer, sultry summer" instead of "It was a queer, sultry summer" to begin *The Bell Jar,* changing the tense and mood of all that followed. So must you decide: Tried-and-true past, or exciting, trendy—but high-risk—present?

TESTS OF TIME

Past tense is the traditional storyteller's medium, the cornerstone of the classic once-upon-a-time framework. The characters have acted out their destinies. The teller has sorted the events and put them into perspective. Readers feel both the comfort and poignancy of expired time. The author is saying, "now that it's all over, let me tell you what happened to Don Quixote," or "this is how fate treated Madame Bovary."

Present tense, on the other hand, imparts a live-camera mood that is relatively new to literary prose, as well as to journalism. Critics call the effect "immediacy": *You are there. This is all unfolding as you read. No telling where things might spin out of control.* Immediacy has all the voguish appeal of live coverage, video gaming, and reality entertainment. And with writers and editors seizing upon it as the Hot Thing, there's enough immediacy out there to rattle the space-time continuum.

Masterly writers like Carol Shields, Jhumpa Lahiri, and J. M. Coetzee have used present tense in a transparent way. The immediacy feels gravitational, not grabby, as their characters explain themselves and escort us through their stories—including through the use of past-tense flashbacks. Others, like Donald Westlake, keep readers on edge with menacing narrators speaking in real-time present.

But in lesser hands, present tense can diminish the spell of storytelling. It can seem affected, breathless and flighty, or just plain flat. Think of the everyday present tense used to describe past events: *So I wait for a bus and go downtown and buy a few things and eat and take the bus home.* Such here-and-now immediacy can make the there-and-then look good.

When present tense describes past events, it is called the "historical present tense," a staple of much contemporary writing. Like everyday narrative, the historical present tense has a natural directness, even a banality that good writers transcend or exploit. The Stuart Dybek story "Que Quieres" (*TriQuarterly* 117), for example, follows two brothers as they return to their childhood neighborhood and confront the Latino gangs now controlling it. Dybek alternates use of a lyrical past-tense background—one brother's ragged history—with taut, present-tense updates of the forward action:

> [Past:] That was the permission—the omen—to start anew as Jimmy Delacroix, to move to New York in the dead of winter and enroll in the Actor's Studio. . . .
> [To present:] *"Que quieres?"* . . . The Disciple removes his sunglasses, as if for emphasis, then rises to his feet like someone tired of sitting, in need of a stretch.

ESCAPING THE BASE TENSE

Whatever the base (main) tense of a story, earlier and later action must be expressed in other tenses. Knowing the grammatical names of these tenses is less important for writers than mastering the sounds of them. The models that follow should help you to leap from a base tense into past or future actions:

Escaping The Present Base Tense:

She fires the shotgun. She has loaded it just minutes before. Tomorrow she will remember nothing. She will have lost all sense of time.

Escaping The Past Base Tense:

He fell wounded. He had never expected her to shoot. Tomorrow they would ask him what had happened. He would have already asked himself a hundred times.

In either case, if the past action goes on at some length, the "to have" auxiliary verbs are usually dropped after two or three sentences to avoid monotony:

The neighbor appeared. She had heard an argument, had feared the worst. But when had it begun? Something seemed amiss yesterday when she spoke to the woman.

For full flashbacks from the present tense, writers commonly jump to the simple past tense, without the "to have" forms:

She fires the shotgun. She has loaded it just minutes before.

(*Flashback*) She was just seven when her father showed her how to handle a firearm. One Sunday morning he took her and her brother to the upper pastures, and . . .

Now she has shot a man. She lowers the weapon.

BLOOD, SWEAT, AND TENSE

Certain authors try to create a wired ambience by using the present tense: "Tonight I slice my arm on the inside of my left bicep," goes a short story in *River City*. Sometimes the effect is like prose on speed, an effect institutionalized by William Burroughs in his *Naked Lunch* (1962). But it grows speedily tedious if the inventiveness flags. A writer cannot simply superimpose the present tense to make a narrative piece sit up; its use has to make some functional sense.

In poetry, for example, the present tense can function as a natural emotive voice, as it has done for millennia in poems of lamentation, exultation, and passion. "Sweat runs down in rivers, a tremor seizes / all my limbs," wrote Sappho of her love trance in the sixth century B.C. But outside of stage directions and soliloquies, storytelling sailed through some three thousand years displaying minimal interest in the present tense—yet suffering from no lack of immediacy. After all, a reader skillfully drawn into the past is as good as sitting in the present.

So what has spurred use of the present tense in recent writing? Some credit the rise of motion pictures, noting fiction's frequent imitations of the forms of the screenplay. You-are-there radio broadcasts might also have played a part, though use of the present tense was still unusual in 1939, when British writer Joyce Cary felt he owed the world an explanation for using that tense in a novel. In his preface to *Mister Johnson,* the story of a charming but self-destructive African clerk at a colonial outpost, Cary wrote that until critical judgment sets in, the reader feels at one with a book's characters:

> [I]f they are in the past tense, he is in the past, he takes a part in events that have happened, in history, over there. . . . But with a story in the present tense, when he, too, is in the present, he is carried unreflecting on the stream of events; his mood is not contemplative but agitated. . . . As Johnson swims gaily on the surface of life, so I wanted the reader to swim.

SPUNK & BITE

Cary saw the present tense as a narrow beam of light that intentionally leaves a vast darkness unilluminated. Its use, say some modern critics, still requires that narrow beam—perhaps an intimate connection with a single character. John Updike did it with Harry Angstrom in the *Rabbit* quartet, and Walker Percy with Binx Bolling in *The Moviegoer.* A number of autobiographical memoirs, such as Kathryn Harrison's *The Kiss,* also beam their way through dark history via the present tense.

Ursula Le Guin told interviewer Amy Sterling Casil that the present—this "special-use" tense—can "freeze" events as if in a single moment of happening or being. Anne Beattie found the present tense a natural way to transcribe quickly conceived images. Anita Shreve recast her manuscript of *Fortune's Rocks* in the present tense to make its nineteenth-century ambience more immediate and less sentimental. And in the opening of their present-tense thriller *Black Horse,* Stephen King and Peter Straub announce their disquieting intent: "Right here and now . . . we are in the fluid present, where clear-sightedness never guarantees perfect vision."

PRESENT (TENSE) COMPANY INCLUDED

Past-tense narratives often include present-tense passages to create special effects. In such cases, the present might be used for emphasis, for general commentary, or to set a stage. It is used to create distance—from the main action (as in flashbacks), the narrator (as with a switch of voice), or the normal state of the characters (as in dreams, interior monologues, and so on.). Sometimes the effect is a strobe-like intensity—past-present-past-present—a potentially jerky style that is not for every writer.

These excerpts offer a glimpse of the many effects:

A prologue, preceding the past-tense narrative:

> All the fragments of the afternoon collect around his airborne form. Shouts, bat-cracks, full bladders and stray yawns, the sand-grain many-ness of things that can't be counted.
> It is all falling indelibly into the past.
>
> (—Don DeLillo, *Underworld*)

Non-conscious state:

> [The fever] burned deeper now. He lost consciousness. And now he floats above the bed, he can see himself. Water rushes from his skin, pooling, it begins to move, it is no longer sweat but ants that crawl out of his pores and swarm.
>
> (—Daniel Mason, *The Piano Tuner*)

Flashback:

> He looked across the lobby, trying to see his father. . . . Roscoe, at this moment staring across time, finds his father sitting in this corner. It is a chilly spring afternoon in 1917.
>
> (—William Kennedy, *Roscoe*)

Commentary:

> The woman at Macy's asked, "Would you be interested in full-time elf or evening and weekend elf?"
> I said, "Full-time elf." . . .
> I am a thirty-three-year-old man applying for a job as an elf.
>
> (—David Sedaris, "Santaland Diaries," *Barrel Fever*)

Intensity, lyricism:

> They kissed delicately. Sleep, my love. Sleep, she repeats to him. He says he cannot sleep; he is too happy. Talk to me, he said. I love your voice.
>
> (—Susan Sontag, *The Volcano Lover*)

[50]

TENSE AND GENRE

One's rationale for using the present tense may be simply that it works (and sells) in a particular genre and is not yet a cliché. So far it seems to work for that breed of giddy urban novel in which characters gad about between meetings, lunches, and liaisons:

> On the first day of our life together (in the office, of course) Adam calls a staff meeting. And as he is telling his account managers about his expectations, I cannot help but think about my own expectations as his foot accidentally finds my leg.
> (—Michelle Cunnah, *32AA*)

It works for disease-of-the-day stories, reading like the writer might not make it to the end. It works for accounts of certain on-the-spot interviews ("He blows his nose and orders a Bordeaux as we begin."). And even in past-tense literary fiction, it works as a change of pace—as stream of consciousness, dream, prologue, epilogue, character-narrated story, freeze-frame event, climactic scene, and the like. (See sidebar, "Present (Tense) Company Included.")

Rationale or none, writers should tread cautiously in such genres as gumshoe detective fiction and apocalyptic sci-fi, where overdone present tense sounds like parody. Romance publishers give the thumbs-down to present tense, claiming reader resistance to anything that dilutes the sense of beginning, middle, and end. As for poetry, only a poem's intent should govern tense. According to the late poet and poetry editor Peter Davison, too many poets are "clinging feebly" to present indicative as a fashionable tense. But judging by the preponderance of that tense in such select anthologies as *The Best American Poetry,* other poetry editors are more amenable to its use.

[51]

And while past tense has dominated the works appearing of late in best-short-story collections, present tense has still been very much present. Those using it have chosen the edgy spouse over the self-controlled one; and in these cases at least, the risky partnerships have worked.

EIGHT

DICTION: WE ARE THE WORDS

"[W]e are the words that tell who we are," wrote Uruguayan poet Eduardo Galleano. He could have been talking about diction, because nothing so quickly defines people as the words they choose from all the levels and shades a language offers. Humbert Humbert, *Lolita*'s urbane narrator, will never be confused with Huckleberry Finn, any more than Don Quixote could emerge from the diction of Sancho Panza.

Diction, or overall word choice, is a partly natural, partly conscious effort for most of us. From such early models as parents, teachers, and peers, we acquire our functional vocabulary and various stylistic choices. Gradually or with a concentrated effort, we embrace certain choices to become, say, plain-spoken, super-cool, or silver-tongued. When our favored diction falls flat with an important audience, we tend to alter it—to put on a verbal costume. "A pleasure to meet you" is the dressed-up diction for an employer. "Yo, wassup?" (or the latest streetwise salutation) goes down with da homies.

For writers, diction is *always* purposeful, always a costume donned for one effect or another. In each new work, it proclaims the narrator's intended personality and point of view. It spins

[53]

Texture / Writing into the Mood

characters out of thin air, shades everything that is spoken about. It sets the mood of the performance and shapes responses to it.

For example, in Graham Smith's novel *Last Orders,* the author's natural, Cambridge-influenced diction is set aside as the novel unfolds through the dictions of its working-class narrators. Among them are earthy Ray and lyrical Vic:

> *{Ray:}* Bernie pulls me a pint and puts it in front of me. He looks at me . . . with his loose, doggy face but he can tell I don't want no chit-chat. . . .
>
> *{Vic:}* [A war ship] would rear up howling and hissing, ice like marzipan on the forward deck, the bows plunging and whacking . . . the swing and judder of steel.

DICTION BY TYPE

As members of a society, we share a common and constantly changing lexicon: thousands of everyday words and idioms, plus the most popular terminology from much-heard subcultures, such as teenage, ethnic, corporate, religious, or rural. As we go outside the shared lexicon, we develop individual patterns of diction according to which subcultural locutions we *habitually* choose. Among dozens of ways to say "calm down," for instance, such habit-based choices might yield:

> *Put a lid on it, for cryin' out loud.*
> *I will not respond to these stressful and unproductive outbursts.*
> *I think you need to, like, channel that negative energy?*
> *You best chill, sucka.*

[54] One's overall vocabulary is usually a blend, hard to categorize as one single type of diction. But key choices can be tracked along

any number of spectrums, including vulgar-to-eloquent and concise-to-verbose. We may hear of good and bad diction, correct and incorrect, but such judgments smack of elitism. Right versus wrong diction has to do only with purpose. High-flown diction might be right for a sermon, but plumb ridiculous for a manual: *Conjoin securely the flare nut with the fitting lest they come asunder.* Not under my sink.

Much of the old class prejudice against "lower" vocabulary has faded, and many writers—perhaps most these days—pepper educated diction with colloquialisms and slang: "Yeah, what an anti-establishment wackjob," wrote Arianna Huffington in *Salon.* And observed David Denby in *The New Yorker:* "When Giamatti goes over the top, he transcends Everyman schmuckiness and attains acting immortality."

Dictions also range along the spectrums of formal/informal, warm/cold, concrete/abstract, and assertive/timid, to name just a few. Scholars document these ranges (including male/female) in a given work, and readers sense them. But authors, as free as gods to choose any diction, must decide which will yield the desired effect.

DICTION AND AUDIENCE: THE RULES

Should authors pump up the diction for an erudite readership? Write down to others? Ape the imagined diction of an audience? Or should art alone determine the diction of a work?

Much depends on the type of writing. In several categories, rules or conventions govern diction as they do other style elements. The unwritten rules of academic writing, for example, decree a diction characterized by complex

[55]

constructions, cautious vocabulary, and passive-voice dryness. One can buck the model, but at the risk of losing credibility and peer status. Likewise, popular media have their own models—some dumbed-down, others bright and inventive. Most family newspapers keep to a vernacular in the pre-teen range of intelligibility. Trend-driven slicks shape diction around fashion blab, valleytalk, gangsta-ese, and other extreme idioms, while fanzine writers adopt one version or another of geekspeak. Television pressures its writers to address the inner juvenile potato.

Writers of literature for actual young people are told *not* to downshift to some perceived juvenile diction, which youthful readers reject. By fifth grade or so, most book-loving youngsters favor the elegance and force of a full-throttle grown-up voice. Consider this passage from a work that middle-schoolers read with ardor:

> Balthamos was slender; his narrow wings were folded elegantly behind his shoulders, and his face bore an expression that mingled haughty disdain with a tender, ardent sympathy, as if he would love all things if only his nature could let him forget their defects.
>
> (—Philip Pullman, *The Amber Spyglass*)

While diction in such genres as romance do sometimes require a nod to audience, literary authors are free to follow aesthetic intent. Whichever dictions rise out of theme, content, setting, character, and so on, are generally considered the appropriate ones in literature.

There is no artistic sellout, however, in echoing the diction of an intended audience—if, in the author's view, it helps make a connection and communicates meanings. A writer like Sandra Cisneros shapes ethnic-influenced diction—"Ay, girl, I'm telling you"—into high art. Even the hard-edged diction of a wave of hiphop novelists, horrifying to some traditionalists, does for its readers what egghead diction does for eggheads: it engages, stimulates, and gives voice to feelings and ideas. Listen to Sister Souljah, who, like gangsta-lit writers Renay Jackson and Shannon Holmes, built an avid following of hip-hop readers:

[56]

> After my hair was butter, I left with Natalie to go check my Aunt Laurie.... We had plans to go to Big Moe's, the local bar and dance set

that be banging on Friday nights. . . . There was never no problem about Big Moe or his bouncers getting in your business. . . . I bet none of these chicks lived in an apartment as laced as Souljah's. When you get a bill in the mail it ain't a "we" thing. When I buy clothes they ain't for "we" they for me. I live for me. I die for me.

(—*The Coldest Winter Ever*)

Still, those who tilt diction to audience face certain pitfalls, among them the appearance of condescension and pandering. When preppies speak in rap, they hip-hop on thin ice. When speech writers feed folksy diction to politicians headed to the hustings, it can backfire with those down-home voters. Columnists ring false when they force their diction to mimic the working stiff's or inflate it in some surge of moral passion.

One interesting technique of diction is to flip it *against* the expectations of an audience. Readers might expect fastidious, curmudgeonly diction in a book defending rigid standards for English punctuation. But in *Eats, Shoots & Leaves,* Lynne Truss frames her case in chatty colloquialisms, with outbursts as unrefined as "argy bargy" and "cock-a-hoop." Concluding one chapter, she remarked that beauty of composition is "not to be sneezed at in this rotten world." And the rotten world—language sticklers included—loved it to the tune of sales in the millions.

THE WRITER'S CHOICES OF DICTION

Ah, those exhilarating choices writers face at the outset of a work! Past tense or present? First-person or third? Omniscient or limited point of view? And now, add the matter of diction.

"Speak, that I may see you," Socrates was said to have told a youth who visited him. How will your fictional characters make themselves seen by their word choices? How will author-as-narrator speak and thus appear? In an intelligent vernacular? With a street-smart eloquence? In a politically correct acad-

[57]

Texture / Writing into the Mood

emese? Should the author's own diction be natural, mixed, or alien?

For writers, the main challenges are to:

Choose dictions that are appropriate to the topic and audience. Breezy slang in a history of smallpox? Ugh. Literary diction in a sports story? Yes, but for sophisticated audiences. (Poetic diction, by the way, in the sense of bower, quoth, dovewinged, and other archaisms, has been pretty much ruled inappropriate for any purpose other than laughs.)

Make the diction authentic or authentic-sounding. Can you create convincing diction for an eighteenth-century British naval commander? Or, as novelist Mark Haddon did in *The Curious Incident of the Dog in the Night-Time,* for a fifteen-year-old math genius suffering from a form of autism? "Write what you know"—or at least what you can research or guess at convincingly—is the rule that applies here. Modern locutions like "have a nice day" should not creep into dialogue of another era unless there's a farcical element at play.

Choose dictions that can deliver intended meanings. Don't box yourself into a type that lacks the nuances you will need.

Fiction writers who work up profiles for each character—parentage, schooling, jobs, travels, etc.—might consider how much of this background will bear on the character's diction. A common pitfall is inconsistency—as when child narrators slide into vocabularies beyond their years, or laconic toughs suddenly wax poetic to get the author's point across. It can also be tricky to deliver visceral meanings in a consistently lofty diction. Novelist Kazuo Ishiguro pulled it off, however, in *The Remains of the Day,* fine-tuning the vocabulary of Stevens, the butler and narrator, to an aspiring-upper-class British English:

> I must say this business of bantering is not a duty I feel I can ever discharge with enthusiasm. . . . One need hardly dwell on the catastrophic possibility of uttering a bantering remark only to discover it wholly inappropriate.

This unvaryingly restrained diction delivered the novel's gut-level feelings—as touchingly as did the profane rant of an ex-con in *How Late It Was, How Late,* James Kelman's Booker Prize–winning novel:

> But it couldnay get worse than this. He was really f***t now. This was the dregs; he was at it. He had f***ing reached it now man the f***ing dregs man the pits, the f***ing black f***ing limboland, purgatory . . . where all ye can do is think. Think. [Asterisks politely mine]

ELEMENTS OF DICTION

Diction colors tone and overall style. Its personality comes from phrases, usages, and grammatical choices, as well as from single words. In her short story "Cakewalk," for example, Lee Smith serves up a southern variety:

> She's always making those cakes. You can see her going through town carrying them so careful, her tired plump little face all crackled up and smiling, those Adidas just skimming the ground.

Dictions can be built also on clichés, circumlocutions, and mannerisms, as Charles Dickens knew so well. But most telling are the

[59]

words themselves, selected from a wealth of options for such qualities as precision, connotation, and association. Should one use *inmate, detainee, jailbird,* or *con?* Every time writers consult a thesaurus or spin alternative words, a diction-related decision is on the line.

Tarquin Winot, narrator of John Lanchester's *The Debt to Pleasure,* is a voluptuary of impeccable tastes in food, with "impeccably correct" diction (as the dust jacket suggests). But Lanchester slowly reveals the true Tarquin through his "poisonously opinionated" vocabulary:

> [T]he menu lies close to the heart of the human impulse to order, to beauty, to pattern. It draws on the original chthonic upwelling that underlies all art.

Chthonic? Doesn't that refer to the dark spirits of the underworld? One begins to suspect . . .

Diction defines a suicidal narrator in "Screenwriter," a *New Yorker* story by Charles D'Ambrosio. Dolorous metaphors meet the slick phrasing of a career screenwriter, as the narrator describes

> a shadow that gave off a disturbing susurrus like the maddening sibilance settling dust must make to the ears of ants. . . . [H]er lips were lovely, the color of cold meat. . . . I'm all bottomed out. I'm down here with the basal ganglia and the halibuts.

To show yourself, to get into your characters and reveal them, be the words. When you've got the diction right, you can look at your story and declare, "That's the only way it could have been spoken." Or you might hear yourself saying, *"Most* felicitous." Or maybe, "Can't word-up no finer." It depends on your diction.

NINE

THE PUNCHY TROPE

When authors wrench language and image out of the literal, they create figures of speech, or "tropes." Metaphors and similes are among the most common figures, along with hyperboles and puns. Although tropes have always been the warp and weft of literature, modern writers have been emphasizing the warp: The more warped, the more attention-getting.

Novelist Salman Rushdie first drew headlines when Islamic fundamentalists vowed to kill him in response to scenes from his novel *The Satanic Verses.* Since then, he has kept our attention with magisterial warps of imagination, including tropes like this one from *The Ground Beneath Her Feet,* describing a rock star's death:

> Meanings beamed down from the satellite-crowded skies, meanings like amorphous aliens, putting out pseudopods like suction pads and sucking at her corpse.

ROPE-A-TROPE CONTENDERS

If you will pull free of Rushdie's suction pads, I will unleash a million-dollar baby of a trope to advance our point. I now ask you to don a pair of imaginary boxing gloves and think of yourself as a free-swinging pugilist. Got it? Good; then you are ready to contend with today's heavy hitters. For when it comes to tropes, many favored writers are going for Sunday punches as well as the old stylish combinations. Call it Friday-night-fight-card-comes-to-language, but contemporary writing abounds with comedic hooks, sarcastic jabs, and hyperbolic haymakers.

When journalists go for the big trope every third paragraph, it brings to mind the famous "rope-a-dope" trope of boxer Muhammad Ali. Ali would stand against the ropes, "rope in" an opponent, and let the "dope" swing wildly, wearing himself out; then Ali would finish him.

To rope a trope can be just as flashy—and risky. For that's how it is in the trope game: Connect, and bask in cheers; miss, and you're flat on the canvas. Here, for example, is a roundhouse punch from Lynne Truss, our friend from the previous chapter. In *Eats, Shoots & Leaves,* her best-seller on punctuation, she suggests this cure for writers addicted to semicolons: "Knightsbridge clinics offering semicolonic irrigation."

Whoops—that one came up empty, didn't it? Such double-meaning tropes, of course, are called "puns," lowest of the figurative blows. Not that Truss has to worry; she delivers enough loopy tropes to delight a world of fans (including me), as with this metaphor:

> [The comma evolved into] a kind of scary grammatical sheepdog . . . [that] tears about on the hillside of language, endlessly organizing words into sensible groups.

BEST TROPE FORWARD

Poets can wave their tropes proudly, staking whole poems on them and winning glory for such figures as "the wind's like a whetted knife." (John Masefield, *Sea Fever*). But prose writers are told that their figures of speech, while stimulating readers, should not call attention to themselves. This may be true in the long run; yet in many contemporary passages the trope is the thing, the signature dish, the bell-ringer—much as it is in our pop culture, conversation, and online chats.

Notice how often, in reviewing a work, critics select tropes as representative excerpts; for example, *New York Times* critic Janet Maslin in describing Walter Mosley's *Little Scarlet*: "One woman in a blue checkered dress is said to have 'looked like a well stacked pile of black pears held in place by a farmer's tablecloth.' " These tropes then become the measure of an author's appeal—one more reason to mind your rhetorical figures.

Today's contenders show their figurative stuff mainly with so-called comparative tropes, such as similes and metaphors. (A simile, you will recall, makes an explicit comparison: *poetry like sludge;* a metaphor implies it: *that sludge heap of poetry.*) Comparative tropes heighten the meaning or clarity of a subject by relating it to something more vivid. When the comparison also tickles the reader's fancy, you've got a winner.

"Her head dropped by degrees," writes Martin Amis in his novel *Yellow Dog.* A bit plain, this action; but here comes the simile to make it vivid: "Her head dropped by degrees, like the resilient jolts of a second-hand." Not only do we see the head tick-tocking downward now, but we can delight in that precise image—maybe even borrow it to impress the lunch crowd.

But can Amis's trope be reused in print? Probably not. A good trope is factory-fresh, unpredictable, economical, and custom-fitted. For all that work—because of it, in fact—the trope has a shelf life of about one use. After that, it joins the family of what author Robert Hartwell Fiske calls "moribund metaphors and insipid similes."

[63]

Is a good trope worth the work? Certainly, as is any locution that regales the reader with fresh images, novel connections, and lucid meanings. It catches the critic's eye. It helps readers remember you. And besides, creating punchy tropes—comparative or otherwise—is as entertaining an activity as will ever occupy us tortured wordmongers. Reading *I'm a Stranger Here Myself*, I could just hear Bill Bryson chortling over his figures: "a man whose prose is so dry you could use it to mop spills"; a gift sweater with "the sort of patterns you get when you rub your eyes too hard."

For better or worse, fun-to-write tropes are going to call attention to themselves. And if the reader gets in on the fun, all is well. Writers have long been entertaining themselves with "extreme" metaphors for extraordinary phenomena: *smash-mouth football, moral black hole,* and so on (see Chapter 3); readers, too, seem to like them. Now, authors are discovering the fun of over-the-top tropes for ordinary things as well. How ordinary? Well, as unexceptional as commas, dry prose, a sweater—or, what Carrie Karasyov and Jill Kargman describe in *The Right Address*: a knick-knack collection that looks "like Bangkok exploded in the foyer."

IS MY TROPE HOT OR NOT?

You may have noticed that Web sites such as "Am I Hot or Not?" and "Rate My Implants" have invited visitors to judge people and their, er, attributes by the numbers. Everything is getting mass-rated these days; so why not figures of speech, or "tropes"?

Long before the Internet, classical critics considered tropes a key measure of an author. Plato, for one, took a pounding for his "drunken" metaphors. And next to creating tropes, what could be more fun than extolling or bashing someone else's? But until RateMyTrope.com gets off the ground, writers may need to appraise their own efforts.

As much as authors adore the figurative darlings of their own imaginations, they must expunge any that are facile, confusing, discordant, or overwrought. The final judgment is how the figure might play to one's intended audience.

Here, I've rated a few tropes using a scale of one to ten, ten being the best. See if you agree. (At the end, I've included several extras for you to appraise on your own.)

"He looked rather pleasantly like a blond satan." (—Dashiell Hammett, *The Maltese Falcon*)

Rating: 9. Three good tropes bring P. I. Sam Spade to life: a paradox ("pleasantly"), a simile ("like . . . satan"), and an oxymoron, or seemingly contradictory statement ("blond satan").

"As he advanced . . . all his [fat] bulbs rose and shook and fell separately with each step, in the manner of clustered soap-bubbles not yet released from the pipe through which they had been blown."
(—Dashiell Hammett, *The Maltese Falcon*)

Rating: 2. Overloaded. Hard to visualize. "In the manner of" and "through which" are out of tune with gumshoe diction.

"[Gangsta-novel writer Donald] Goines's pimped-out plots gleam like custom rims on an Escalade." (—Elvis Mitchell, *The New York Times*)

Rating: 7. Good image if you've seen a gangsta-ish Cadillac Escalade SUV fly by on luminescent wheels. The trope's consonance (*p*'s, *n*'s) and rhythm suggest gangsta rap.

[65]

"Norah Jones and her foot soldiers are organic, grass-fed artists taking back the castle from the injection-molded, poly-blend popbots." (—Sasha Frere-Jones, *The New Yorker*)

Rating: 5. Passionate, but a huge load of metaphor even for pop-music buffs.

FOR YOUR APPRAISAL:

- "The penguins tottered and clucked and dived, slipping off the habitat rocks like amiable hams but living under water like tuxedoed muscles." (—Alice Sebold, *The Lovely Bones*)

- "I felt like an undeveloped photograph that he was printing, my image rising to the surface under his gaze." (—Janet Fitch, *White Oleander*)

- "[Michael Moore is] too eager to throw another treated log onto the fire of righteous anger." (—David Denby, *The New Yorker*)

- "Within minutes of my first kiss I was stripped like a squid . . . and something inside me hardened, turned into a chunk of cement. A girl becomes a comma like that, with wrong boy after wrong boy; she becomes a pause, something quick before the real thing." (—Lisa Glatt, *A Girl Becomes a Comma Like That*)

- ". . . [a woman who is] now thin enough to tread water in a hose." (—Eric Garcia, *Cassandra French's Finishing School for Girls*)

- "[The album] sounds like the work of someone who's recently had her heart pressed into service as an ashtray." (—Alex Pappademas, "Happy Woman Blues," *Spin*)

- "[M]y reflection . . . stopped and stared—hair on end, mouth agog in idiotic astonishment—like a comic book character konked on the head with an anvil, chaplet of stars and birdies twittering about the brow." (—Donna Tartt, *The Secret History*)

SPUNK & BITE

- "Today's gourmet Bobos want a 48-inch-wide, six-burner, dual-fuel, 20,000 Btu range that sends up heat like a space shuttle rocket booster turned upside down." (—David Brooks, *Bobos in Paradise*)

- "But [John] Daly is as sober as an Amish librarian."

- "...Melania Knauss, who is just so damn centerfold beautiful she ought to come with staples." (—Rick Reilly, *Who's Your Caddy?*)

- "The unease...seemed to rise with the turbulent brown river swollen by the April rains, and in the evenings lay across the blacked-out city like a mental dusk which the whole country could sense, a quiet and malign thickening." (—Ian McEwan, *Atonement*)

- "Sex, it seemed, was as forgettable as a dinner out; set asideable as a floppy disc. Relationships got remembered: they were there on the hard disc." (—Fay Weldon, *Worst Fears*)

COMEDIC TROPES

Suddenly everyone's a comedian. And audiences are in love with the comedic trope, especially the stand-up style inspired by film and television entertainment. In writing, efforts range from high wit (truth through wit) to what Dorothy Parker called "calisthenics with words"—the hard-working wisecrack. The genre dubbed "chick lit" abounds with such calisthenics, to the delectation of its readers: "One good kiss from the right guy still makes you more radiant than a year of dermabrasion." (Janice Kaplan and Lynn Schnumberger, *The Botox Diaries*)

If attention is what you want, such outrageous tropes are a way to get it. And few writers can resist all the nutsy, trope-ready phenomena out there: the latest cosmetic torture, misbehaving celebrity, or failed enterprise. Troping such topics to the edgy boundaries is one way to avoid clichés; the trick is to not alienate your audience. Admirers of gentlemanly British tennis player Tim Henman, for example, must have been put off when the London *Daily Express* said he was "as likely to win Wimbledon as Osama bin Laden," even if the rest of the tabloid's readers guffawed.

Some critics like to disparage comedic tropes as "jokey," even as they borrow several of such jokes to juice up their reviews. Jokes may no longer be funny at airports, but the last I heard they still play to the general reader. Just ask Dave Barry, whose jokey hyperboles have come by the planeload: "Compared with the Japanese, the average American displays . . . all the subtlety of Harpo hitting Zeppo with a dead chicken." (*Dave Barry Does Japan*)

When not quoting comedic tropes, critics are often showcasing their own. They are writers, after all. Of an actress playing warrior Guinevere in the film *King Arthur,* reviewer Josh Tyangiel of *Time* cracks, "[Keira Knightley] wears so much blue war paint that she looks like the world's most ferocious Smurf."

LITERARY LAUGHS

Can jokey be literary as well? Well, here's just one trope from Raymond Chandler's *Farewell, My Lovely,* part of the Library of America's collection of Literary Classics: "He looked about as inconspicuous as a tarantula on a slice of angel food."

This hyperbolic simile, one of many from the master, dates from the 1930s. Jokey, you see, wasn't always a liability. After all, the jokey trope was validated in the third century by Cassius Longinus, Greek rhetorician and presumed author of *On Great*

Writing, a classic of criticism. Defending hyperbole, Longinus said that "[a work's] actions and passions that bring one close to distraction compensate for and justify every boldness of expression." Noting that "laughter, too, is a passion which has its roots in pleasure," Longinus cited this one-liner: "His field was shorter than a Spartan's letter." (*Bada-boom!*) Longinus did warn, however, that "the use of tropes, like all beauties of language, always tends to excess," as if the writer were drunk.

TROPE CONTROL

In *A Poetry Handbook,* Pulitzer Prize–winning poet Mary Oliver also cautioned against excess, focusing on the images contained in tropes. She warned that too many " 'jolts' of imagery may end up like a carnival ride: the reader has been lurched, and has laughed—has been all but whiplashed—but has gotten nowhere." Such excess occurs in prose, too—especially in genres like travel writing, where so many unfamiliar experiences beg to be compared with known, concrete images. The temptation often leads to "conceits," or metaphors that are extended beyond one or two comparisons. In his generally moving *Prague Pictures,* John Banville describes the title city as a place where

> time lays down its layers like strata of rock, the porous lime-
> stone of the present over the granite of the Communists over
> the ashes-and-diamonds of the Hapsburgs over the basalt of
> the Premyslids.

Some conceits work, each trope adding something meaningful; others are maddening. If my earlier boxing conceit maddened anyone, be tolerant—I'm teaching! And be thankful that I stopped the fight after a few rounds, because almost any metaphor can be

[69]

extended, as they say, to the gates of doom. Why? Because all particulars of the universe share at least some qualities—both a shoe and a geranium can be new, old, bright, owned, loved, deteriorated, forgotten, discarded, and so on. Most astonishing is that all possible comparisons have not been exhausted and never will be—not even the punchy ones. Readers, however, can be exhausted faster than a shoe gets scuffed. In general, heed the type of advice given to comedians: Know when to step off the trope.

Trope management affects the texture of a piece—how figurative and lyrical it will be. It does the same with fictional narrators and characters, giving them a texture based on the natures and amounts of their figures of speech. Astrid Magnussen, fictional narrator of Janet Fitch's *White Oleander,* speaks in extravagant tropes that sometimes fall just short of parody. For example, "we stared out at the city that hummed and glittered like a computer chip deep in some unknowable machine, holding its secret like a poker hand," and "I was bricks sewn into the hem of her clothes. I was a steel dress." Extravagant, yes; but such tropes perfectly reveal the texture of Astrid's mixed-up-yet-resilient soul. On the other hand, in his novel *Disgrace,* J. M. Coetzee portrays the literary soul of David Lurie with barely a metaphor in sight, the austere texture suggesting Lurie's desolation and ultimate despair.

Writers naturally want to compete and be noticed, and most will feel they can equal the punchiest or most hilariously warped tropes in contemporary writing. Indeed, they should go for the big warp in any genre that welcomes it. But one last trope is worth bearing in mind: In the weaver's art, a controlling hand— a discerning and restraining hand—fits the warp skillfully into the weft.

SPUNK & BITE

Word

LANGUAGE—AEROBATIC
AND INCANDESCENT

TEN
HOW TO LOOT A THESAURUS

Who can resist? Open a good thesaurus such as an authentic *Roget's,* and feel the urge to appropriate—to *lay hands on, pluck, plunder,* and *loot* its bounty of words. I confess that the aptly named thesaurus (from the Greek for "treasure house") unleashes my own rapacious urge to snatch the goose that lays the golden synonyms.

Ah, but snatcher beware. Writers as diverse as Simon Winchester (*The Professor and the Madman*) and novelist Stephen King warn that words plucked from a thesaurus—especially as intended synonyms—are ill-gotten and bogus. Don't open the thing in the first place, they advise, since its so-called synonyms are but closely related words that have taken on their own nuances. By blindly plugging in these undefined words, a writer risks being off-target, arcane, pretentious, or downright ludicrous. So they tell us.

The Oxford-educated Winchester, writing in *The Atlantic Monthly,* tarred *Roget's* for "our current state of linguistic and intellectual mediocrity." In eighteen pages of what thesaurus lovers would call a rant, he argued that *Roget's* seduces the masses with an easy solution to word choice; and yet,

[72]

because the users are ill-versed, and because the book offers no help at all in discovering what anything means, the word chosen with each *presto!* is often wrong. . . . Each time such a wrong is perpetrated, [language] becomes a . . . measure more decayed, disarranged, and unlovely. And that, I suggest, is why all *Rogets* should be shunned.

Winchester allowed that the thesaurus might be used to jog the memory or solve a crossword puzzle; "but one never, never relies on it to help with the making of good writing."

So decreed Winchester. And King seconded the motion in *On Writing,* in effect telling readers to toss the great treasury—with its 330,000 terms organized into 1,075 categories—to the nearest junkyard dog.

But hold on just a minute.

ROGET'S MUNIFICENT GIFT

If I were to throw any thesaurus to the (virtual) dogs, it would be the type that is often bundled with word-processing programs—the low-rent, censored, lazy-person's list of pedestrian synonyms. Talk about seductive. I pity anyone who might judge the splendor of true thesauruses by these click-and-fix aids for office memo writing. They have nothing to do with the beneficent genius of a retired doctor named Peter Mark Roget.

Roget (1779–1869) had the sort of restless intellect that allowed him to solve London's water filtration problem, invent the log scale for slide rules, and organize an immense collection of words into categories, according to the *ideas* they represent. The first such collection, *Roget's Thesaurus of English Words and Phrases* (1852), launched a fleet of editions that he and his successors improved upon over the decades. It also prompted a host of (generally inferior) imitators bearing Roget and "thesaurus" labels, many of them simply alphabetized lists of synonyms.

The longevity of the categorized (classified) *Roget's*—which has endured for more than a century and a half—confirms its value to word seekers. In contrast to an A-to-Z dictionary of synonyms, where one seeks a *mot juste* by slogging door-to-door through rows of words, a genuine *Roget's* charts the word on a comprehensive map of ideas. One zooms in from thematic provinces to thematic villages to thematic streets, where the words and phrases live. Using the vast index, one can spring from an approximate idea (say, *bright*) directly into a neighborhood (*light*) teeming with such luminous terms as *incandescent, effulgent, lambent,* and *opalescent.* Or, via the classified arrangement, users can wander thematic roads toward their destinations, choosing well-marked trails (*flash, glow, radiation, reflection*) and exploring unknown and thrilling language (*rutilant, coruscating*) along the way.

That, I think, is the magic of *Roget's* for writers: Traveling from theme to theme, directed by cross-references and other clues, one lives among word families, discovers Shangri-las of exotic terminology, beholds clashes of synonyms and antonyms, and finds adventure even in misused words. Shun this wonderland of expression? A writer would have to be mad, unhinged, moonstruck to do so.

THESAURUSES TO LAY ONE'S HANDS ON

Here's a selection of printed thesauruses to be found in bookstores or libraries. (Later editions of these titles may also be available.) At least one quality thesaurus belongs within an arm's reach of any up-and-coming-writer.

Some online thesauruses are also listed below.

Roget's International Thesaurus. Fifth edition: Robert L. Chapman, editor. New York: HarperCollins, 1992. 1141 pages, indexed. Sixth edition: Barbara Ann Kipfer, editor. New York: HarperCollins, 2001. 1280 pages.

The HarperCollins versions are heirs to the original *Roget's.* For the fifth edition, Chapman overhauled the Victorian categories, building a postmodern framework (1,073 categories) for 325,000 related terms. Included are many special lists, such as "Gods and Goddesses" and "Manias and Phobias." The sixth edition features further updating, additional lists, and hundreds of quotations.

Bartlett's Roget's Thesaurus. First edition: Roger Donald, editor. Boston: Little, Brown, 1996. 1415 pages.

With some 325,000 references in 848 main categories, *Bartlett's* is organized by concept, like *Roget's.* Its classification has been overhauled, its contents Americanized. Quotations from *Bartlett's'* vast archive illustrate selected words. The massive index is all-inclusive, covering all the entries, synonyms, lists, and quotes.

Roget's 21st Century Thesaurus in Dictionary Form. Second edition: Princeton Language Institute, editor; Barbara Ann Kipfer, head lexicographer. New York: Dell, 1999. 957 pages, paper.

A good choice as far as relatively portable, A-to-Z thesauruses go. Includes a conceptual index to seventeen thousand main-entry terms and an impressive 450,000 synonyms (many repeated) associated with them.

Random House Webster's College Thesaurus. Revised and updated by Fraser Sutherland. Original editors: Jess Stein and Stuart Berg Flexner. New York: Random House, 1997–98. 792 pages, paper.

With a medium-range number of main entries (twelve thousand), this A-to-Z thesaurus is bountiful in synonyms and antonyms (some four hundred thousand), mindful of new terms, and distinguished by thousands of word-in-context sentences and discussions of usage, even of offbeat words. (If you mean *awry,* don't use *cattywampus,* "a midwestern locution for diagonally opposite.")

[75]

Word / Language—Aerobatic and Incandescent

Webster's New World Roget's A–Z Thesaurus. Fourth edition: by Charlton Laird; Michael Agnes, editor. New York: John Wiley, 1999. 894 pages.

A synonym dictionary with frequent "synonym studies" and brief definitions to aid usage. The classification scheme presented up front is of limited use. Features include cross-references, antonyms, and special lists.

A few thesauruses have enduring Internet presence, though at this writing none matches the quality of the best print volumes. Web addresses change, but the following and other examples can be located using key words on a search engine such as Google:

Wordsmyth Dictionary-Thesaurus (*www.wordsmyth.net*).
Definitions, synonyms, and related words on one site featuring some fifty thousand headwords. Neither the latest nor largest in terms of vocabulary, but the site's clear distinctions, advanced search capabilities, and quick links help users to pin down words. Free registration is required.

ARTFL Project: Roget's Thesaurus Search Form
(*http://humanities.uchicago.edu/orgs/ARTFL/forms_unrest/ROGET.html*).
One of several sites offering Project Gutenberg's digital transcription of *Roget's* (1911 edition, supplemented in 1991). Searchable by headword or from the full text.

Merriam-Webster Online Thesaurus (*www.m-w.com/home.htm*).
Allows quick look-ups of synonyms, related words, and antonyms included in *Merriam-Webster's New Collegiate Thesaurus.*

The Visual Thesaurus: A Dictionary of the English Language
(*www.visualthesaurus.com or thinkmap.com*).
In this otherworldy thesaurus, related words float around chosen terms; when clicked on, they become the center of a shifting matrix—an ingenious presentation echoing and aiding the mental process of word association. A sample trial is available on the Internet; desktop and online versions are offered at modest prices.

TIPS FOR WORD GATHERERS

Before venturing to the hinterlands of words, writers might want to consider these tips from a weathered *Roget's* traveler:

Understand Roget's' *possibilities.* Use a thesaurus to

- discover more fitting or more forceful words;
- find those good words you can't quite recall;
- avoid repetition of words;
- escape clichés and worn modifiers;
- help describe the so-called indescribable;
- refine your intended meanings (via related concepts); and
- simply luxuriate in the plenitude of language.

But understand Roget's' *limits.* Do not look to the thesaurus to supply newly minted phrases, fresh and surprising uses of a word, or unique imagery; it can't provide these things by itself. Nor can a traditional *Roget's* tell you how felicitous (or ridiculous) a word will be in your context, although some recent thesauruses offer hints. When you loot a treasury, the loot doesn't tell you how to spend itself. For looters, that's the creative part.

Before embracing an unfamiliar word, look up its definition and usage in a good dictionary. *Roget's*-bashers can't imagine that anyone would take this *duh* of a step. Look-ups can be tedious, but words looked up are words attained, whether or not they turn out to be *mots justes.*

Don't fish in the categories, swim in them. The thesaurus organizes each category by nouns, adjectives, verbs, and adverbs. Don't cast in only one pool for the most creative solution. Dive into several listings, then do the same with the nearby antonyms. Looking for a fresh way of describing wild laughter? Look under *lamentation,*

Word / Language—Aerobatic and Incandescent

where such terms as *bawl, keen,* and *roll in the dust* are ready to rollick.

Don't grab all the words that fit. As a writer seeking blurbs and other publicity, I confess that I've been obsequious, unctuous, groveling, fawning, toadying, and truckling at times; but shoot me if I ever use all those synonyms again in a sentence. So many juicy words crop up for a concept, and we want them all. But we have to make a choice based on nuance, texture, rhythm, and sound—keeping in mind our audience's frame of reference.

Search your brain as well. Don't truckle to the genius of Roget. As you consider the thesaurus's suggestions, keep pumping your own synapses for related words and offbeat associations. One stimulating trick is to flip the thesaurus to a section that has nothing to do with your original category. The terms here may suggest figurative alternatives to a synonym. For example: I want to communicate the brightness of light; I flip (randomly) to the "Violence" section and find such terms as *savage, brutal, barbarous,* and *scorching*—one of which might be more forceful and telling than, say, *glaring.*

Use new and/or older editions. While new editions may have added handy features and thousands of new terms, many of these terms may also be already-outdated colloquialisms, such as *yukky.* I like the option of resuscitating quaint terms—even quaint slang words like *monstrotonous*—from older editions.

Take chances. Yo, this ain't Oxford, where word bunglers fear towel whippings and social snubs. Stick your thumb into that thesaurus and pull out a plum. If now and then you end up with a prune, you'll have learned something—and both you and English will survive.

Recently the novelist Alan Furst weighed in against *Roget's,* saying that rather than succumb to "thesaurusitis," he chose to repeat an apt modifier (*billowing*) throughout his entire book. Okay, so you can't always find an alternative for a good word, even in the mighty seas of the thesaurus. But don't throw out the boat with the bilge water. For all writers there comes a time when, abandoned by their muses, adrift like the Ancient Mariner, they pray for the wallop of a favorable word—a word to billow their sails and push them along. For thousands of authors, *Roget's* has answered that prayer; and if it pushed them in new and unintended directions, so much the better for readers.

Word / Language—Aerobatic and Incandescent

WORDS WITH MUSIC
AND *SPLOOOSH*

BZZZZ . . . RRRIP . . . NYEEEOW. That's the sound of a writer's brain at work. When it comes to shaping experience into words, the brain box needs all the rhetorical tools it can hold. One of the oldest such tools—yet as contemporary as steel-cutting lasers—is onomatopoeia, a form of "sound symbolism." Like all power tools, it must be well honed, fitted to the job, and used with extreme caution.

So, you there—clicking the keys, gulping your coffee, braying at the muse as your computer burps and hums: Watch carefully as we throw the onomatopoeic switch.

But—*screech!*—hold on, we've already thrown it, haven't we? A word such as *click* or *gulp,* mimicking the sound of the thing named, is exactly what rhetoricians mean by *onomatopoeia,* from the Greek term for "word-making." The word *onomatopoeia* itself should bring a swoosh of nostalgia to those who learned to jangle its six syllables in college. On-o-mot-o-pee-ya. Textbooks presented it mainly as a poetic effect, invariably warbling these lines from Tennyson's "The Princess": "The moan of doves in immemorial elms, / And murmuring of innumerable bees." Or maybe you got the Robert Browning sample, from "Meeting at Night": "A tap at the pane, the quick sharp scratch / And blue spurt of a lighted match."

Aesthetically, poets do get the most out of the device, given the oral tradition of poetry and its marriage of sound and meaning. But those who command both the *whomp* of onomatopoeia and *ka-ching* of royalties tend to be prose stylists—Tom Wolfe the most ear-splitting of all:

> The fan overhead went *scrack scrack scraaaaccccckkkkk*. Grover Washington's saxophone went *buhooomu-hoooooooom. . . . Thra-gooooom! Glugluglug* went the toilets. . . . And then the *tuck-atuckatucka-tuckatuckatucka* [of spoons beating ice cream cups] began. (—*A Man in Full*)

Other writers cashing in on "echoic" words, as they are also called, include graphic novelists such as Mike Allred (*Madman Comics*), who *sprongs* noisy, uppercase words across his panels in the best tradition of comic book creators. His *bams* and *blams* are standard fare, but most of his onomatopoeia is a blast or two ahead of the lexicon: "SPTANNG! THOOM! FTASK! NYAASH! BTHUP! FTASK, FZASK, THROCK! SPLOOSHH!" (*G-Men from Hell*) Not that graphic novelists invented loopy onomatopoeia. James Thurber was there some time ago: "Tires booped and whooshed, the fenders queeled and graked," he wrote in one of his sketches.

Just as words like *gargle, gobble,* and *squawk* appear in everyday speech, onomatopoeia finds its way into almost any extended piece of writing. Such casual use helps animate a passage without calling attention to itself. For example, in Nadine Gordimer's "Safety Procedures," a *New Yorker* short story about a horrendous plane ride, teeth "chatter," the pilot "gabbles," sick people "gurgle," and a heart "thuds." Here the onomatopoeia emerges naturally; but when writers deliberately nail a precise sound, one feels the difference—as with Wolfe's *chundering* ventilation system or Don DeLillo's *wallop* of the wind on sheets hung to dry. How those images resonate!

RESISTING THE PRIMAL URGE

In his *Essay on Criticism,* Alexander Pope encouraged fellow poets to let the onomatopoeia rip: "[W]hen loud surges lash the sounding shore, / The hoarse, rough verse should like the torrent roar." No one has to lash writers, however, before they'll use an echoic effect. Like readers, writers love the sounds of words—sometimes a little too much. A linguistic element as basic as onomatopoeia is naturally seductive. How basic is it? Some linguists suggest that speech began as imitative sounds (iconic) as opposed to utterances merely symbolizing the things described. Though somewhat creaky now, this so-called bow-wow theory is reflected in the imitative *choo-choos* and *quack-quacks* of toddlers (and their parents).

People acquire hundreds more echoic words as they zip, glug, and spule their way through adolescence and beyond. Each linguistic culture comes up with its own mimicry: Germans hear *bimbam* when bells ring. To the French, le pooch barks le *ouâ-ouâ*.

Perhaps owing to its very simplicity, echoic language gets heavy-handed when writers use it in obvious ways, especially in poetry. Certain clichéd sounds attach to certain subjects, and must be shaken loose. For example, it would seem that the sound of bells can be described only in so many ways, especially after Poe took it to the limit in "The Bells" with such famous lines as: "To the tintinnabulation that so musically wells / From the bells, bells, bells, bells." After this, can anyone wring fresh onomatopoeia out of bells? Good writers still find ways, as does Gabriel Gudding in "Foundry" (*American Poetry Review*). In this evocative poem, a fallen brass bell suffers wounds and humiliations as it struggles along a road seeking relief, "its swollen clacker . . . donking against fire hydrants and curb." A ding may be one thing, but a donk is clearly another when you're a down-and-out bell.

ONOMATOPOEIA FOR THE SEASON

Mud-luscious. Puddle-wonderful. Can you feel, in these phrases from e.e. cummings's poem "In Just-spring," that squooshy, soggy time of year?

Spring may be the ultimate prompt for sound symbolism, particularly onomatopoeia. Words gush forth to mimic the season's chirps and gurgles, or to whisper their qualities:

Thunder, boom, rumble, flash, crash . . . pitter-patter, plash, plink, plunk, splish, splash, dribble, drip . . . ooze, squish, babble, bubble, burble . . . croak, click, cluck, cheep, tweet, twitter, coo, chirrup, drone, bleat, croon . . . whump, flap, whish, whistle . . . crack, pop, vroom, slurp, sizzle.

But these are merely the standard-issue echoes of spring delights. Your job is to go out, put your ear to the world, and gather fresh variations on the theme.

BASHES, FLASHES, SNIVELS AND SNORTS

Here's another twist on sound symbolism and writing: Linguists have observed that words containing similar sounds often express

[83]

similar meanings. Experts find it easier to describe the phenome-non—commonly called "phonesthesia"—than to figure out its origins. But wherever it came from, there it is, for writers to use.

Phonesthemic words contain sounds we somehow associate with qualities of subjects, rather than the sounds they make. Think of *slime, slurry, sludge,* and *sleaze,* for example, all suggestive of ickiness. Other phonesthemic groups include those nasty *sn*-words (*sneer, snarl, snide, snitch*), the forceful *-sh* gang (*bash, dash, rush, crush*), the shining *gl*'s (*gleaming, glittery*), and wee *-ee*'s (*eensy, teensy*).

Why do these groups exist? Did facial expressions give rise to the sounds?

Linguists regard such simplistic answers as bogus, but there's nothing phony about phonesthesia itself. Many hundreds of words, from profanities to endearments, fall into such groups. Phonesthemic words can lend feeling and texture to a line of po-etry, a character's name, a scene, an editorial, or even an ad. Con-sider these *sh-* words describing the debris of a Philadelphia wharf, circa 1765:

> [U]nderfoot lies . . . shreds of spices . . . , splashes of Geneva gin, . . . oranges and shaddocks fallen and squash'd. (—Thomas Pynchon, *Mason & Dixon*)

If there are ways to animate debris, this is one of them—just as phonesthesia's cousin, onomatopoeia, can make the jungle cry from the pages of *Into the Heart of Borneo,* by droll amateur or-nithologist Redmond O'Hanlon:

> I awoke at dawn, to the *dididididi* call of the Grey drongo . . . ; the chatterings and muttering and babbling of un-

seen Babblers . . . ; the flutings and whistlings and cat-calls of hidden pittas or bulbuls or cuckoo-shrikes . . . ; and the distant hoot of a gibbon.

Whether you awake tomorrow to the *creee* of the seaside or the *bling-bling* of the mean streets, listen to the sounds of life, the telling ones, and capture them for their re-creation in words—not only to reproduce what was heard, but to hint at what was felt.

TWELVE

COINING THE *BONNE* LOCUTION

Today's big American dictionaries contain about four hundred thousand "formations," or words and word combinations; *The Oxford English Dictionary* checks in at almost seven hundred thousand. That's a lotta words, especially when you consider that Shakespeare's entire body of work boasts a vocabulary of only twenty thousand. How many more words do we need for our own *oeuvres?* Shouldn't we exploit the inventory before rolling out new vocabulary? You'd think so. But it doesn't work that way. Usage rides roughshod over the established lexicon. It constantly tweaks old words into essentially new meanings and coughs up new formations. Why? Because humans are irrepressible namers, and life provides an endless supply of things to name: new things, old things seen in new ways, new combinations of things, and imagined things.

We burbling humans invent terms not only to identify things, but also to style our expression or be first or cleverest at naming something. Writers do it in the interest of precision, entertainment, recognition, and even duty: the world expects its authors to show some flash in the art of naming.

Are you ready to deliver?

WRITERS AND NEOLOGISMS

A coinage, or "neologism," is a new word or word combination that someone deliberately creates. Corporations crank them out regularly, as do fecund young minds on campuses and street corners; authors are responsible for untold numbers. Shakespeare himself is said to have invented some 1,500 of the words he used, among them *grovel, hobnob,* and the ever-popular *puke.*

Every day, journalists tag new trends with coinages, like *metrosexual* for straight men who enjoy facials and interior design. Copywriters neologize to herald the next big thing, tech writers to delineate the latest gizmo. 'Zine authors and bloggers neologize like word bunnies, or at least propagate new words from the subcultural breeding grounds.

Storytellers, too—especially those inventing fantasy worlds—create new word formations, and even whole vocabularies, to serve their stories. J. K. Rowlings's *quaffle* (a ball used in the game *quidditch*) isn't any more likely to enter common parlance than Rudy Rucker's *suckapillar* (genetically engineered cleaning bot). But often the neologisms break out, as did Robert Heinlein's *grok* (deep understanding of someone) and George Orwell's *newspeak* (propagandistic Big Brother language). Rowlings's *muggle* (a person with no magical powers) is likewise speeding its way into the dictionaries.

At times, authors neologize to distinguish things so ordinary that they have gone unnamed. Apparently no one had an English word for "going about on foot" until 1791, when William Wordsworth coined the noun *pedestrian.* Did it help pedestrians get right of way? We don't know; but the coinage is decidedly of the utilitarian type: logical, made to serve, often influenced by Latin or Greek. More often, when writers name the unnamed,

[87]

there's an element of play afoot. Oscar Wilde is said to have coined *dude* as a combination of *duds* and *attitude*.

Too much play, of course, distracts authors from the triathlon of writing—getting it down, getting it right, and getting it published. But when play delights readers as well as author, everyone wins. We would like to think that Edgar Allan Poe rang up a rare moment of glee when he coined *tintinnabulation* (the sound of bells) in 1831; readers certainly have loved it. John Irving probably had fun coining *undertoad* (fear of tragedy) in *The World According to Garp* (1976), even if it played into the tale's dark motif; the word (originally the phrase *Under Toad*) became a favorite of the book's audience.

If you write cultural or social commentary, you have the right—nay, the obligation—to mint terms for movements, trends, and groups. In 2001, writer David Brooks coined *bobos* (from *bourgeois* and *bohemians*) to describe former social rebels who have become well-heeled and self-indulgent. Some such coinages stick, and some even attach to their creators in perpetuity, as has *pseudo-event* to Daniel J. Boorstin, the late historian and social observer.

WRITERLY MATTERS NEEDING NAMES

Rockumentary. Digerati. Bling. American subcultures pour out coinages like slot machines gone berserk, and the literary subculture contributes its share. Yet for every *slush pile, back story,* and *bodice ripper* minted within the writer's world, some other writerly subject—often dolorous—cries out for an established (and perhaps cathartic) name. Here are several such entities, awaiting coinages for you to create (as practice) and share with fellow *wordaholics*:

- A terse rejection note

- A great idea you forgot to write down

- The joy and pain of seeing a friend's work published before your own

- An inept muse

- The agent who won't communicate, loses your manuscript, and bills you anyway

- A draft of a poem that you loved yesterday, but hate today

- The almost-right word

- An activity performed as an excuse to avoid writing

- A merciless editor

- A news event that renders your completed manuscript out-of-date

- A passage you know you should cut from a piece of writing, but can't

- The act of turning your book face-out on bookstore shelves

COINING FOR THE HAPPY CLICK

Generally speaking, it is not glory that drives one to neologize. Rather, one does so mainly for the sake of felicity—that happy *click!* when language perfectly fits idea. Such clicking coinages add joy to the works of Lewis Carroll, Dr. Seuss, James Joyce, and other zealous neologizers. Good coinages make reading a skosh more fun—whether they occur in the literary heights, where Joyce Carol Oates coined *pathography* (a biography dwelling on negative aspects), or in the tabloid swamps, the spawning grounds for terms like *sexaholic.*

[89]

After all, most coinages are no more than "nonce" terms, meant for a single occasion and perhaps for a couple of laughs. Only the most useful or popular are gathered into book and Internet collections, and fewer still make it into the dictionaries—thankfully, or we'd be driven mad by them; it's bad enough when a writer goes coinage-crazy in a short piece, as unstoppable as a mad punster. As a rule, neologisms should be limited to those best serving the purpose of the work—and only the cleverest at that.

If the purpose is to entertain, however, the model collection is comedian Richard Hall's *Sniglets* series (1984–1989), which presents "words that should be in the dictionary but aren't." Snigleteers, who still abound, create cute-sounding words for the unnamed entities of everyday life; e.g., *slurm* for the ick on a soap dish, and *bovilexia* for the urge to moo at cows. Such arguably needed terms are also called "word fugitives," a theme Barbara Wallraff has pursued in her *Atlantic Monthly* columns on language.

While most coinages fall short of immortality, writers of all types have produced neologisms that are gifts to the language as well as to their readers—terms we truly needed, such as Joseph Heller's *catch-22* or sci-fi writer William Gibson's *cyberspace.*

And speaking of cyberspace, imagine how many coinages are emerging this minute from the multitude of fevered online chatpersons. A staggering thought, but one that suggests a testing arena for a writer's neologizing skills.

HOW TO NEOLOGIZE WITH THE BEST OF THEM

To sharpen those word-making powers, you might try a few of these standard methods of forming neologisms. In all cases, the coinages should be quick-witted and clear; not labored, not arcane, and not timid.

Combining. Combine existing words or word parts (prefixes, suffixes, etc.) to make a new compound or other formation. You might go for a funny incongruity or a play on existing words: *granny-bashing, eco-thriller, hottitude.* An *Esquire* movie critic coined the term *insta-chum* for a couple stranded in shark-infested waters. Try something with the suffix *-ectomy,* which denotes excision of whatever precedes it.

Shortening. Clip away parts of existing words, as in *'do* (hairdo), *'tude* (attitude), or *'roid* (steroid). The intelligence community's clippage for spies is *humint* (human intelligence). Think of words containing more syllables than they need to deliver their meaning—then chop 'em down to create something catchy.

Blending. Blend one or more words into a new one; or blend clipped words with existing ones. Also known as "portmanteaus," blend words include *spim* (from *spam* and *instant message,* or *IM*), *cremains, glamazon,* and *bridezilla. Lollapalooza* is clipped to make *guiltapalooza* (excessive remorse), as used in a *Buffy the Vampire Slayer* TV script.

Borrowing. Borrow or recast foreign words and word parts: *überagent* (a super agent, such as Michael Ovitz); *fauxmage* (fake cheese). The Spanish suffix *-ero / -era,* which indicates that someone is employed at something, is a good starter for you worderos and worderas.

Epynomic naming. Turn well-known proper names (real or fictitious) into nouns, verbs, adjectives, etc.: *mega-scrooge; Dorothy Parkering.* When Anna Kournikova was the "it" girl of tennis, another player called the sport "over-Kournikova-ized." What would your name suggest as part of a coinage?

Word / Language—Aerobatic and Incandescent

Creating. Make up an entirely new word, as Lewis Carroll did with *chortle* and *burble* for *Through the Looking-Glass* (1871).

Carroll advised neologizers to "take care of the sounds, and the sense will take care of itself"—a thought worth considering as you test your word-coining talent here (see "Writerly Matters Needing Names" sidebar) or at some point in the *triauthorlon* that never ends.

THIRTEEN

WORDS WITH FOREIGN *UMAMI*

The Japanese word *umami* (oo-MOM-ee) has all the qualities of a foreign term worth borrowing: It is rich in meanings, easy to read, and not bettered by an English equivalent. A Tokyo scientist coined it in 1907 to indicate a "fifth taste"—a deliciousness or savoriness that goes beyond the four basic tastes: salt, sour, sweet, and bitter. Never mind that the scientist found *umami* in monosodium glutamate, that head-rattling flavor enhancer. The word itself connotes something mystical, some quintessential quality, a perfection.

Though not yet assimilated into American English, *umami* has reached Yankee shores in connection with food. A writer for *Wine Spectator* referred to a coconut lime soup as "a caldron of umami." And a chef who liked the sound of the word proclaimed himself "The Swami of Umami" on a T-shirt.

But now the word is ready for use in a literary or metaphorical sense, to evoke the quality of exquisiteness wherever it is found. Surely an adventurous writer like yourself can conjure a fresh application; or perhaps from your world travels, experience with a foreign language, or word collecting, you have some other cross-cultural gem ready to drop into in an English sentence. We are talking about an infrequent act here—a dash that spices the

[93]

Word / Language—Aerobatic and Incandescent

whole. But thinking about even a single use of a non-English term brings up three options:

- To use the term unencumbered by a translation, assuming your core audience knows it, can dope it out from context, or will at least appreciate the look and sound of it.
- To use the term and translate it for the reader, as best you can and in as few words as possible.
- To not use it in the first place, heeding Rule 20 of Strunk and White's *The Elements of Style*—namely:

Avoid foreign languages. . . . Some writers . . . from sheer exuberance or a desire to show off, sprinkle their work liberally with foreign expressions, with no regard for the reader's comfort. It is a bad habit. Write in English.

A PENCHANT FOR "NATIVE" SPEECH

Such admonitions to stick to one's own words seem a day late when it comes to American English—roughly three-quarters of which consists of "loanwords," or terms that were borrowed from some 120 non-English languages and naturalized over the centuries. (A word that becomes naturalized by frequent use loses its italics; often it also takes on local spelling and other characteristics—for example, "vamoose," which comes from the Spanish *vamos,* meaning "let's go.")

What exactly does it mean to "write in English"? Does it mean using only those terms granted citizenship by dictionaries or other authorities? Such has not been the English or American way. For the *umami* of the Anglo-American lexical broth, we can thank all those language users smuggling foreign terms into the vernacular over the centuries.

Fair enough, however, is Rule 20's advice against mad "sprinkling" of foreign words—a trait sometimes seen among polyglot show-offs or young writers fresh from a *Wanderjahr* through Europe. One can even nod here and there at H. W. Fowler's 1908 rant on foreign words in *The King's English,* which warns against forced applications, misleading literal translations, and ignorance of a term's foreign nuances.

But with hindsight, one can brush off Fowler's claim that "all words not English in appearance are in English writing ugly and not pretty"; for we now see that his "ugly" examples—*employé, Schadenfreude,* and *penchant,* to name three—include some of our most successful borrowings or assimilations since 1908.

Fowler maintained that the case against foreignisms was not a "counsel of perfection" to be dismissed by all but the most fastidious writers. He argued that there was simply no excuse for substituting unfamiliar or semi-familiar foreign terms for known English ones—not for precision, not even for ornamentation. Fowler's warning knell, along with Strunk and White's, is sounded by some conservative mentors today, as if a terrorist might ride in on a foreign term, or English writing might suffer trade deficits in a global economy. But English is protected by the preponderance of Anglo-Saxon (or so-called native) words in daily speech and literature, even if they comprise a minority of the national lexicon.

As to deficits, there is no worry today: Spoken in one fashion or another by some 700 million people on the planet, English is the world's most-studied foreign language, and the official language of more countries than any other. English words and Americanisms, to the despair of some governments, are probably the most borrowed; the Japanese alone have borrowed and adapted some twenty thousand. We can certainly absorb the odd *umami* in return.

STYLE AND FREQUENCY OF FOREIGNISMS

Most style guides agree that italics should be used at least for the first appearance of foreign terms in a piece of writing, along with the original diacritical marks and capitalization. But use roman type for proper names and passages of foreign text.

Roman is the preferred typeface for "assimilated" foreign terms—those your dictionary authority prints in roman type as main entries, or "head words." Follow the dictionary's guidance regarding diacritical marks for these terms.

How often should foreignisms be used? Try this generalization: Up to three borrowings per article or chapter should be stimulation enough for most readers, unless terminology itself is your subject. This three-word guideline includes terms borrowed for their distinctive meanings and those simply substituting for threadbare English equivalents. Remember that such substitutes—say, *dernier cri* for *the latest thing*—also wear thin, often faster than their English counterparts.

REASONS FOR USING FOREIGNISMS

A *fatwa* against foreignisms, driven mainly by fear of extremes, condemns to non-grata status thousands of expressive terms that might be put to work in English writing. Yet, a *barbaridad* (fearful amount) of good reasons can be found for using artfully chosen foreignisms. Here are a few of them:

SPUNK & BITE

Precision. Suppose you sought a noun meaning "a code of silence and secrecy sworn to by oath"—to refer, for example, to a corporation's code of internal affairs. Is there an English word more precise, whether grimly or playfully used, than the Italian *omertà?* "They think I broke the Kennedy code of omertà," wrote *New York Times* columnist Maureen Dowd, who considered the term familiar enough to her readers that she used it without translation.

Connotation. A foreign term like *omertà* carries special associations, unique undercurrents of meanings. In *The New Yorker,* James Surowiecki described a period of "monetary *omertà*" at the Federal Reserve, playing on the term's dark Sicilian origins to suggest a malicious pattern of obscurity and deception. Once it makes headlines, a foreign term blazes through world journalism—and, as a vogue borrowing, may soon burn out or become naturalized. "Greenspan's real legacy has been to bring glasnost to central banking," Surowiecki wrote, using the once-explosive, now naturalized Russian word for government openness.

Freshness. One of the overlooked reasons for going foreign is to make the ordinary sound delightful—not to impress readers, but to entertain them, introduce a little flippancy, relieve the fug of banality. Think of all those German and Yiddish words that tickle the American ear with their *schm-* and *schn-* sounds. Right now, the popular term for a lover of eating is *foodie,* but the lip-smacking German term *Feinschmecker* gets my vote.

English may be one of the most versatile languages, but it is not always the most lyrical. To American ears, *prestamo interbibliotecario* sings like an Italian tenor; *interlibrary loan* does not. In a classical tongue, the humdrum of cyberspeak suddenly thrums majestically: *Inscriptio ordinatralis* is the orotund version of *internet address,* according to Latin enthusiast Konrad Kokoszkiewicz.

[97]

Piquance. Here is how William F. Buckley Jr., another Latin enthusiast, explained to a correspondent his passion for untranslated non-English words: "[D]elicately used," he said, "they do bring little piquancies and with them, well—*aperçu* [quick insight] which, because they are extra-idiomatic, give you a fresh view of the subject."

Elsewhere in the Buckley collection *The Right Word,* he compares the deft foreign word to the unexpected jazz chord that pianist Thelonius Monk would strike at the right harmonic moment—different, perhaps bizarre, but not something a listener would want stifled.

Tone. Even in the most unlikely genres, the refined ear enjoys a touch of the tony—of a language not spoken by every palooka. Cheering foreignisms in sports writing, Indiana columnist William Meehan wrote:

> In a *Sports Illustrated* article about a boxing club . . . [A. J.] Liebling brings into play not only French but Latin . . . *succès d'estime, mouchoirs, in absentia* and a poetic transposition of *non compos mentis.* . . . And he does so sans explanation, against the recommendation of journalism's leading style manual.

Synonymity. A foreign term provides an option to repeated words when tired English synonyms won't do. Imagine a sentence like this: " 'A body of works comes from an artist who has worked and worked hard,' she said, speaking of her own works." Using "*oeuvres*" for the last word sounds better.

Atmosphere and characterization. Hemingway did it with Spanish, Stanley Elkin with Yiddish, Nabokov with four or five languages:

splashes of foreign words and dialogue for authenticity, to put the reader in the scene, to animate characters. What I long recalled from William Styron's *Set This House on Fire,* read ages ago, were bursts of untranslated Italian evoking the high-pitched Neopolitan atmosphere: " *'Bella Vista,'* he roared, *'Tutti i conforti . . . panorama scenico . . . prezzi moderati!'* "

Generosity. When we interpret a reader's world through the sensibilities of another culture, we present a gift, ideally one worth unpackaging. Like gifts once brought from abroad (before everything could be bought everywhere), these special terms can be savored, treasured, and collected—say, as Mario Vargas Llosa did with *morbidezza,* an Italian word for a softness "that sounds lustful even when applied to bread." I expect authors of foreign-themed literature to slip me a few such gifts within their stories, or feel the sting of my peevishness.

REASONS TO HESITATE

What reasons are there to withhold these treasures, to deny readers such gifts as *karma, cognoscenti, frisson, kiosk, macho,* and *mojo,* all now assimilated into English? Why muzzle the Sturm und Drang? Here, in addition to the pitfalls mentioned by Fowler, are some common objections to using foreign terms:

Imprecision. We hear it said that "the French have a word for it"— but it's often more like three or four words. In many cases, when you're tempted to use a foreign term, chances are that English has a more precise one within its enormous, flexible vocabulary. If "literally" is what we mean, as in, "she took my wisecrack literally," why use *au pied de la lettre?*

Improper tone. Though they appear successfully in every genre, foreignisms are simply off-pitch in certain works. They may be out of sync with the narrator, characters, or atmosphere of a story—or all wrong for its audience. It's a matter of ear.

Bafflement. A page into *The Wasteland,* T.S. Eliot baffled many readers with four lines of German ("*Frisch weht der Wind*" . . .), followed by some French and Italian. But bafflement has its place in high poetry—sometimes that's part of its intrigue. Great poetry assumes the reader's willingness to labor over its mystery in exchange for a soul-stirring payoff. Elsewhere in literature, however, long and untranslated foreign passages will be skipped, and probably cussed at.

Sheer pedantry. One who uses foreignisms mainly for show will show up mainly as *un cojudo a la vela*—an ass at full sail, as they say in Spanish.

Ignorance of nuance. It takes moxy to use a newly encountered term when only its literal meaning and perhaps one figurative use are known. According to an American columnist, Chinese journalists call a barely legal act a *cabianqiu*—the term for a Ping-Pong shot that just catches the table. Handy word—but does it suggest a sly thing, or a deplorable one, or what?

Foreign slang is especially precarious, shifting according to time and place, offensive to one and not another. One can favor slang terms that have achieved some universality, like the French *merde* or Spanish *cojones,* but such terms may have lost much of their punch in the process.

Erroneous usage. The fear of looking foolish or fraudulent haunts every writer who uses a foreign term without fluency in its source language. Chances for misuse are legion: Transliteration is a nightmare from which no one escapes unchallenged, not to mention the difficulties of understanding case, tense, plurals, and agreement. "She met a dude *fatale*," sounds cool; but there is no applying *fatale* to anything masculine, and *fatal* loses its Frenchness, as Wilson Follett warned in *Modern American Usage.* There he argued that "foreign phrases should be used only when no native equivalent is to be had."

But here we have argued otherwise; because equivalence in meaning does not always mean equivalence in feeling or delight—in stimulation—for our too-often understimulated readers. Because writers, who *always* face the possibility of looking idiotic, must muddle along anyway, relying on howls and adjustments over time to make things right.

WHERE TO FIND APT FOREIGN TERMS

Authors usually don't go fishing for foreign words and phrases to store in their notebooks. Were they to do so, a few dips into sources like *The Oxford Dictionary of Foreign Words and Phrases* would net enough lunkers for a lifetime. Instead, writers tend to gather the most useful foreignisms from travel, study, multilingual friends—and from the borrowings of other writers.

From journalists come good borrowings for describing contemporary events; creative literature turns up eclectic choices. The first writer to borrow an apt term gets points for originality, but it is perfectly legit to re-borrow someone else's borrowings if they suit your context. After all, borrowings are just words entering the lexicon as words always do: by pass-along.

When you do encounter a juicy term, try checking its form and usage in an English reference like the Oxford collection (which features some eight thousand words in more than forty languages) or a dictionary in the original language. If you can't find the term or even read the original script, take a chance anyway. Shakespeare did, made a few mistakes, and ended up okay.

USABLE TERMS: A SAMPLING

I. From newspapers and magazines:

- *fiza* (India). The street and marketplace buzz before an election.

- *catastrofista* (Italy). Someone who makes a catastrophe out of everything.

- *suji* (Japan). The strong "line" or "spine" of philosophical reasoning necessary to make decisions.

- *yoik* (Lapland). To chant in a glottal, singsong, yelping manner.

- *mammoni* (Italy). Sons who never leave the comfort of home and pampering mothers.

- *noyrwws* (Finland). Quiet pride in the past, humility toward the future.

- *gecekondos* (Turkey). Hastily built apartment buildings on the edges of a city.

- *dietrologia* (Italy). The art of finding dark ulterior motives behind ordinary-seeming decisions.

- *mutumba* (Kenya). Bales of secondhand American clothing sold in markets.

- *bidoon* (Kuwait). Stateless noncitizens.

- *tutela* (Colombia). A citizen's writ for quick judgment on a violation of rights.

- *Dalits* (India). The former "Untouchables" caste. *Dalit* means "ground-down" or "downtrodden" in Hindi.

II. From literature:

- **shpatziering** (Yiddish). Shameless sauntering: "... shpatziering all over India looking either for her soul or some swell new herbal tea." (—Stanley Elkin, *Mrs. Ted Bliss*)

- **interesnoe polozhenie** (Russian). Literally "interesting condition," a euphemism for something far more consequential, such as pregnancy: "[N]either [of them] remembered to dope procreation, whereupon started the extremely *interesnoe polozhenie*." (—Vladimir Nabokov, *Ada*)

- **chato / chata** (Portuguese). An annoying bore: " 'The world can do without *chatas* like Teresa Caravalho,' he said." (—Robert Wilson, *A Small Death in Lisbon*)

- **neican** (Chinese). Restricted, internal: "It is a restricted book—it is *neican*." (—Paul Theroux, *Riding the Iron Rooster*)

- **pur** (Greek). Fire. "*Pur:* that one word contains for me the secret, the bright, terrible clarity of ancient Greek. How can I make you see it, this strange harsh light ... ?" (—Donna Tartt, *The Secret History*)

MONOLINGUAL READERS

What about those understimulated readers we mentioned earlier? How many of them understand even the most common foreign words and expressions? Americans reared in the U.S.A. are famous for their monolinguism, and the withering of foreign languages in our schools and colleges assures more such notoriety.

Yet I believe that the majority of modern readers—awash in global communications—will appreciate the stretch, the learning

[103]

op, of good foreign terms besides *pokémon.* As for those who would rather swallow a *mofongo* whole than sample a linguistic savory from the global kitchen, I point to the sensation *mofongo* evokes before one learns it is a spicy, Puerto Rican dumpling the size of a cue ball. Even for those who pass by words with *umami,* there is the pleasure of their scent.

Force

STIMULATION BY ANY MEANS

FOURTEEN

DIALOGUE TAGS WITH OOMPH

When dialogue needs to be attributed to someone, writers use what is called a "tag" for the job. *Said* is the usual tag. Harriet *said;* she *said.* Or *asked,* or *replied.* How many more are there? A study turned up some six hundred different tags in just one hundred novels by twentieth-century British and American authors. Authors averaged a range of about fifty in each novel.

But pretend you never heard that; because most writing gurus tell you to use no tags—or, if necessary, a single one: *Said.*

"Well, this annoys me," I say pointedly. "This *annoys* me," I hiss. "This annoys me!" I trumpet through cupped hands.

Why? Because I don't like rigidity in writing advice, the rules of attribution included. And this is not just an authority problem. I admit that the writing pros are 95 percent right when they lay down rules such as these for tagging dialogue:

- *Elmore Leonard:* "Never use a word other than 'said' to carry dialogue. . . . Never use an adverb to modify the word 'said.' " (—"Writers on Writing," *The New York Times*)
- *Stephen King:* "The adverb is not your friend. . . . I insist that you use the adverb in dialogue attribution only in the rarest

and most special of occasions . . . and not even then, if you can avoid it. . . . [And don't shoot] the attribution verb full of steroids." (—On Writing)

So maybe they are 99 percent right. But it's the 1-percent-wrong part that intrigues me, because that's where some of our most commercially successful writers live; because that's where the thrill of risk and reward comes into play; and because rigidity can hamstring an idea on its way to expression: say, the idea of someone sounding off—as Martin Amis tags it in *Yellow Dog*—liverishly.

DRY STYLE

When should writers be frugal in their tags, shunning adverbs and limiting themselves to the triad of *said, asked,* and *replied?* Generally, when a speaker's manner of expression is already clear. What makes it clear? Such elements as context and content of the dialogue, narrative description, and the speaker's character. For example, *said* is attribution enough in this passage:

> A cry of terror broke from Dorian Gray's lips, and he rushed between the painter and the screen. "Basil," he said, looking very pale, "you must not look at it." (—Oscar Wilde, *The Picture of Dorian Gray*)

For Dorian to have "gasped" or "said anxiously" would have been redundant, a telling instead of showing, a denial of the reader's imagination—all that bad business.

Some writers try to avoid tags altogether, even the simple *said.* This trend has spread throughout writers' workshops, where minimalist and screenplay-like styles are imitated and produced.

Force / Stimulation by Any Means

Many writers today—and some editors—feel that dry attribution tags indicate professionalism, whereas more dramatic tags shout "amateur." And little wonder, given the tendency of inexperienced writers to overdo the inflated verbs and adverbs. A single *cachinnated lachrymosely* can give attribution a bad name.

AVOIDING SWIFTIES AND OTHER HOWLERS

A lively attribution verb or adverb can punch up key dialogue, make it more precise. But the pitfalls are many. One must avoid the labored, clichéd, and unnecessary—and at all costs, any trace of a pun. Punning tags—such as the one used in the sentence *"Fire!" yelled Tom alarmingly—* are known as "swifties," after the adverb-heavy Tom Swift adventure series. You'll find thousands of them on swifties-themed Web sites. A few appear among winners of the annual Bulwer-Lytton atrocious-writing contest hosted by San Jose State University, to wit: " 'My left eye has been slowly shifting over to the right side of my face!' she floundered." (Brian Holmes)

DRAMATIC STYLE

Yet there are those writers unafraid of putting some oomph in attribution. They dare to use adverbs, as well as such assertive tags as *spat* and *brayed*. And not every such writer becomes the butt of editorial hilarity or a candidate for atrocious-writing awards (see the "Avoiding Swifties and Other Howlers" sidebar).

Take, for example, the writer of these tags: " 'Shoo!' said Mr. Dursley loudly." . . . " 'No,' she said sharply." . . . " 'I know that,' said Professor McGonagall irritably."

This writer also has her characters snarling, snapping, wailing, and croaking—and doing so coldly, heavily, glumly, sleepily, and so on. But then, what does J. K. Rowling know? Her books have only sold a few hundred million copies in some forty languages. Rowling even breaks the rule that says characters can't hiss unless their dialogue has sibilant sounds. " 'No!' Harry hissed," she writes—and, sibilance or not, the "No!" goes down as hissy.

If such robust attribution should be limited to children's literature, however, Danielle Steel and the buyers of more than 370 million copies of her novels seem unconvinced. Steel tags her dialogue with gusto. Shake just one of her novels (in this case, *Mirror Image*), and out like confetti fall such attributions as:

> "You must come with me," Victoria answered fiercely. . . . "Religion," she smiled mischievously. . . . "I think that's disgusting," she said heatedly. . . . "Neither can I," he laughed. . . . "Yeah," he grinned at her. . . . "You cheated," she accused.

Primly, blithely, miserably, mysteriously, vaguely, soothingly, nervously, cautiously, discreetly, and frantically—thus do Steel's characters chide, moan, wail, and bluster their way through their dialogue.

THE CONFIDENT TAGMEISTER

Stephen King and others blame inflated tags on lapses in confidence—the fear that otherwise a speaker's tone and intent won't come across. Writers should address this fear (after writing their first drafts), and sort out the tags that seem excessive. But excess cannot always be measured against the austere tenets of writers' workshops. Sometimes the author's particular tone, or the genre, or the readers' expectations, call for a vigorous attribution style.

[109]

Force / Stimulation by Any Means

As I flip through shelves of novels, I find occasional, pumped-up attributions to be perfectly welcome clues as to how characters dished out utterances to one another. Salman Rushdie does not strike me as a writer lacking in confidence; but within four pages of *The Satanic Verses,* his characters have "conceded," "admitted, "promised," "thundered on," "said jovially," and "yelled suddenly" what they had to say. With due respect for Elmore Leonard's reasoning that such "intrusive" verbs and adverbs can distract the reader (he especially hates *suddenly*), in the hands of a riveting storyteller like Rushdie they seem only to drive the dialogue, like an emphatic drumbeat.

Often, because speech is nuanced in ten thousand ways, a descriptive verb or adverb is simply a good idea. In an award-winning short story, for example, Hester Kaplan wrote: " 'Cold as hell in New York,' she said hoarsely, as though clots of snow were lodged in her throat." Absent the adverb *hoarsely,* I'd have had to conjure the sound of a snow-clotted throat—which I can't do without choking. Emphatic tags can also provide dramatic counterpoint as they interweave with neutral ones. In this passage from Fay Weldon's novel *Worst Fears,* Alexandra faces Leah, her deceased—and deceiving—husband's colluding therapist:

> "You prurient old cow!" shouted Alexandra. . . .
> "I understand your anger," said Leah.
> "No one understands my anger!" shrieked Alexandra.
> "This session is at an end," said Leah.

DIALOGUE TAGS THAT MADE THE CUT

How many zesty dialogue tags are killed by editors? While the shocking numbers may never be known, we can be sure that flocks of the most passionately composed attributions have perished by the blue pencil. Take heart, however, in this selection of live ones that have made it into works of accomplished writers:

Vladimir Nabokov: *observed calmly, observed slyly, enigmatically observed, commented good-naturedly*

John Irving: *said miserably, said despairingly, bellowed, wailed, screamed, roared*

Alexander Theroux: *giggled, sneered, yawned, brayed*

James Thurber: *spat, growled, barked suddenly, asked thickly, said triumphantly*

Mary Higgins Clark: *shrieked, screamed, sobbed, yelled, asked abruptly, said hoarsely, fiercely*

Charles Palliser: *stammered, urged, breathed, faltered, said ironically, laconically, equably*

Maeve Binchy: *said casually, mildly, hastily, asked companionably, haughtily, suspiciously*

Patricia Cornwell: *muttered, wept, bragged on, blurted out, inanely said, cautiously went on*

Nicholas Sparks: *relented, confessed, protested drowsily*

Jan Karon: *crowed, whistled, bellowed, commanded*

Sandra Brown: *amended, drawled, squeaked, chorused, retorted defensively, asked belligerently, teasingly*

Janet Daily: *hooted, hissed, taunted, raged, challenged, scoffed, emphatically agreed, perversely had to add*

Force / Stimulation by Any Means

BOTTOM LINES

In melodrama, farce, parody, and other tongue-in-cheek genres, dialogue tags can be part of the fun. Go nuts with them. Find fresh terms in the thesaurus—and not just those listed in the "Communicating Ideas" category—to stretch into verbs of expression. For example, from a term in the "Moisture" section of *Roget's:* " 'I think I've had too much to drink,' he *marinated* to the ambassador."

Outside of such lighthearted genres, allow yourself an occasional, juiced-up attribution for clarity, emphasis, or nuance—*unless* it

- repeats what's already clear;
- calls too much attention to itself;
- is one too many to bear;
- goes against your spare style; or
- makes you feel amateurish, and for good reason.

As author Barnaby Conrad pointed out in *The Writer* magazine, feel free to use descriptive tags when something is said in a manner that contradicts the words—"when a character speaks, as they say in theater, 'against the line' (*viz:* 'I love you,' he said savagely)."

Remember that you can avoid forced speech tags with "action tags"—brief clauses detailing the action that accompanies the dialogue. Instead of the awkward, " 'Go, girl,' she thumbed-up," you can write: "She raised a thumb. 'Go, girl.' " Or: " 'Go, girl,' she said, raising a thumb."

And speaking of thumbs-up performance, if you command an audience anything like Rowling's or Steel's—why then, tag your dialogue just as ululatingly as you damn please.

FIFTEEN

ENALLAGE: A FUN GRAMMATICAL GET

Among talk show producers, the corralling of a hot celebrity or headline figure is known as a "get." President Clinton was a get during the Monica Lewinsky scandal. Monica was a get. Gets are gotten by "get specialists." And who in the entertainment industry cares that *get* is traditionally a verb? Or who, when calling something "the new fabulous" cares that *fabulous* made its name as an adjective? All this shifting of function is just more fun (to roll out another shifted noun) in a fun world.

Writers, in their never-ending quest for fresh locutions, can get some gets of their own by taking advantage of this rhetorical effect. Grammarians call it "anthimeria," "functional shift," or "enallage" (a broader term, but my preferred pretty one); it amounts to the turning of nouns, verbs, and adjectives on their functional heads to produce novel usages. Something like this:

So how can questy writers enallage their way to the big Fresh? On that little how, we could noun and verb you all day.

Okay, I'll admit that's a lot of enallage—and not everything can be stood on its head without a horrific flump. Not all at once, anyway. But in a language amenable to enallage, just about every word seems poised for turning. This grammatical shifting (also called "conversion" or "functional variation") accounts for tens of

[113]

Force / Stimulation by Any Means

thousands of common usages, especially in journalism. Think of the verb *rewrite,* and how easily it shifts to a noun ("he submitted a rewrite") or an adjective ("he entered rewrite hell").

Why do words keep shifting function? Well, why shouldn't they, considering that users are the ones shifting them, and that words should serve users—not the other way around? Shifting is broadly embraced in the ever-flexible English language, though sometimes a sudden shift is like a scream of gears.

An English word does not come to us labeled as a "noun" or "adjective" or any other part of speech. This sobering fact is underscored by Bryan Garner in *Garner's Modern American Usage*—a magisterial work for language lovers. Only when a word is used in context does a functional label make sense, notes Garner; however, habits of usage give words the appearance of fixed roles.

Among Garner's examples are words traditionally thought of as nouns—*limo, mayor, box-office*—that newspaper writers have shifted into slangy verbs: "George will be *limoed*"; "He's been *mayoring* in Boston"; "[The film] . . . out-*box-officed* 'Jurassic Park.' " I offer two other examples, this time from the sports world, where functional shifts are as common as hockey brawls—and just as popular with fans. First, from a piece by Kevin Gleason in the Middleton, New York, *Times Herald-Record:* "Matsui . . . *inside-outed* the double down the left-field line." (italics mine) For those keeping score, that's an adjective shifting into a verb. It happens every day in the major leagues, known enallagically as "The Bigs." The second example comes from Mark Wood in *Golfonline:* "Try to *die* the ball into the high side of the hole." (italics mine) Here the verb *die* was shifted from its usual intransitive function to transitive, enabling it to act on a direct object (*ball*). Energetic and useful, this form is now part of the golf lexicon (it refers to the ball's momentum "dying" at the hole).

OUTING THE DISCONNECTS

Do we die the language with all this enallage? No, not our organic, surprise-loving English language. Though a few shifts may raise some, er, aesthetic issues, many help keep our communications playful and engaging. Very few undermine clarity.

One can barely find an English word that has not undergone some functional variation. Often, over time, the variation displaces earlier terminology, proving more economical or precise. To *out* someone, for example, has displaced—who can even remember what heap of words? Most shifting occurs gradually, without fireworks; but when the shift is conspicuous, as in mass communications, it can cause all sorts of excitement.

Disconnect, for example, is an insipid verb that only a utility company can brandish with any force. But toward the close of the last century, *disconnect* became a hot noun. In every corridor and throughout the mediasphere, someone was saying, "We've got a disconnect," with the accent stylishly on the first syllable.

And there it was: the little frisson people derive from bending the language. Perhaps in some minds *disconnect* was simply short for *disconnection,* the preexisting noun. Word clipping has always been stylish in the vernacular: witness *fab, terrif,* and *the diff.* But something else was going on—some bold stroke, some power usage—similar to what happens when a hotel executive calls a branch start-up "a new build" (as opposed to a "rehab"), thus transforming a banal verb into a trendy noun.

Why is "*a disconnect*" still more fun to say than "*a disconnection*"? What makes a functional shift appealing? Is it the power play? The rebellious edge of new and unauthorized usages? Does it have to do with who first makes the shift? Or simply with how snappy

[115]

Force / Stimulation by Any Means

and unexpected the shifted word sounds in context? Certainly the effect merits a heed from writers. A functional twist, and *bada-boom!*—a word gains cachet. It's like turning a baseball cap backward—or, when it really works, like an electron shift among atoms. A media star says, "there's no quit in that guy," and the verb *quit* explodes as a noun in ten thousand sports and business locutions. Masters Tournament golfers who "gutted it out" were said by enallaging sportscasters to have "no quit" and "no *give-up*."

USES OF ENALLAGE

Enallage, or "conversion," is one of those devices we use daily to spark expression, but without considering its dynamics:

- "I'll money you," we joke to some would-be borrower, shifting the usual function of the noun *money* to a verbal one.

- "That'll cost you five large," we say smartly, yanking *large* from its adjectival hangout to serve as a noun.

- We read a bumper sticker aloud—"I *heart* New York"—and the quirkiness of the noun-turned-verb induces a chuckle.

- Or we shift a word from the verbal to the nominal sense: "By the time he left, I needed a good *swear*"—which is more emphatic than "I needed to swear a lot."

Emphasis is what enallage can give us; it draws reaction by shifting the function of a word from that of its usual part of speech to an uncharacteristic function, thereby thwarting the predictable. Some enallage is likely to enter your writing naturally; but now and then an intentional shift gets the desired effect. Examples of such effects include:

SPUNK & BITE

Lyrical force. In many of her evocative poems, Elena Karina Byrne creates startling verbs from such unlikely nouns as *bellboy, patience, quayside,* and *brûlée.* One such poem begins:

> Can I, for a moment?
>
> Dada you to accord something light
> first, sweet you and slow
> you as a canoe, to window you and murmur
> you . . . (—"Sex Mask," Chelsea 76)

Authenticity of dialogue. In the slang of rebel subcultures, shifts be cool—as in *smack* for heroin, *blow* for coke, *kill* for marijuana, and other verbs-turned-nouns. Members of the campus culture have tended to "pig" on noun-to-verb shifts—"Like, don't *crumb* on me, dude; I gotta *book* for the test soon as I *meal.*" In police-procedurese, the officers "good-cop-bad-cop" the perps, and the perps "lawyer up."

Vernacular punch. Prose at any level can get a boost from vernacular shifts, as from an interjection (*whoa!*) shifting to a noun:

> If it's a quick, potent, mind-bending shot of Whoa you seek—and I'm talking about pure Whoa here, the good stuff, undiluted by extraneous gadgets or CGI cityscapes—I give you *Primer.* (—Mike D'Angelo, "Movies," *Esquire*)

Energized proper names. Any name can be made to function as a verb. Adding the suffix *-ized* is one way, but a functional shift is more dynamic:

> "Halloween would have been harrypotterized this year in any case. Now it's been osamaed too." (—"All Hallows Eve, 2001" [Editorial], *The New York Times*)

Coinages for nameless entities. Shift a word's function to denote something unnamed, and voilà—a needed coinage. Philosophy professor Daniel C. Dennet, for example, has introduced *bright* as a noun referring to a person with a naturalist (as opposed to a supernaturalist) world view. He himself is a bright.

Force / Stimulation by Any Means

New grammatical functions for words that need them. Many words, especially new terms, have yet to develop multiple grammatical functions. *Paper,* for example, already functions as noun, verb, and adjective (*the paper said she papered the wall with paper rejection slips*); but *plastic,* as plastic as it might be, won't stretch into a verb by itself; someone had to help it along with deft enallage, as did author/blogger Lee Klein in "Foiled Plots": "Ever since my mother pressed and plasticked my umbilical cord, I've been a collector."

Many intentionally shifted words function best as one-time (or "nonce") devices, used for effect rather than to revolutionize the language. Most words retain their traditional functions for a reason: people like the way they work. So play with enallage, but don't get so shifty that your sentences no longer recognize themselves.

DOWNSIDING INTO JARGON

While shifting is an inventive and often overlooked way to achieve novelty, it also has its downsides. Novelty too often takes the place of elegant vocabulary; and of course not all novelty scores a hit—some of it positively gags discerning readers. Writers inventing or trying out new usages have to weigh their attention-getting value against their turn-off potential.

That negative potential is rarely greater than in the business world, a breeding ground for enallage-spawned jargon. In the ad slogan "We help you to office. To office better," the new verb *office* seems right out of a *Dilbert* cartoon—as does the verb *resource* in the slogan "Resource what you like, the way you like, with Novell Directory Services."

The verb *repurpose* (as in *repurposing the organization*) is the product of yet another shift that offends sensitive eardrums these days—and never mind that it was Shakespeare who originally shifted *purpose* into a verb. (In the Elizabethan era, functional shifts gushed forth like hot springs.) The Bard used *proverb* and many other nouns as verbs, and still packed 'em in at the Globe.

Abrasiveness aside, the proliferation of enallage-based jargon is in keeping with the natural evolution of language. As usual, the question for writers is one of audience. Business people tire of their vogue words; they can only "partner" and "right-size" so long without hungering for aggressive new verbs, including former nouns. If you write for these people, go ahead and purpose your rhetoric to them.

And speaking of the business world, here's a classic case of enallage: When a credit agency identifies a deadbeat debtor, the nonpayer is referred to not merely as a "bad risk" or "bad person," but as a "bad." Shifting the adjective *bad* into a noun is like saying, "once a bad, always a bad, and bad through and through." And before long, without the *grip, scratch,* or *flow* (all shifted verbs referring to money) to pay up, that bad could end up a certified *crazy.*

Force / Stimulation by Any Means

SIXTEEN

INTENSIFIERS FOR THE FEEBLE

Intensity—oh, to achieve it! To intensify one's writing, to punch it up, make it engaging, drive it home. To wield words like axes "for the frozen sea inside us," as Franz-the-Man Kafka intensely phrased it.

All along we've been talking about intensity in one guise or another. And always, the enemy has been the tendency of words to grow feeble with overuse. But now we come to a rhetorical device whose name should give hope to every dull, worn, weak, and cowardly locution:

The intensifier.

Intensifiers are modifying adverbs meant to amplify the qualities of other modifiers (and sometimes the action of verbs). If something is good, then *awfully* attempts to boost—intensify— that quality to *awfully* good; similarly, "*so* small"; "*very* exotic"; "*really* flew." You'd think intensifiers would be *just* perfect for writers. But what do we hear from modern authorities? "Stay away from the things."

Here's the problem: Writers are expected to come up with vocabulary that packs its own intensity—with words like *fractious* (very irritable) and *gravid* (pretty pregnant). Otherwise, writers might as well be any bozo, intensifying feeble words with monotonous profanities—every *freaking* other *freaking* word—or with the stock intensifiers typical of everyday conversations (especially mobile-phone conversations): *very, really, so, extremely, all, definitely, actually, seriously, pretty, wholly, quite, totally, absolutely,* and so on.

Such intensifiers are supposed to jack up the ordinary adjectives and adverbs that everyone has handy—*nice, great, fast, cute, incredible,* etc. Thus do we intensify "nice" in, "Have an *extremely* nice day." But because everyone uses them all the time, the intensifiers themselves can become as dead as the dead weight they're trying to animate. Even seventeenth-century intensifiers that seem colorful to us today—as in "*clean* starved," "*passing* strange," "*shredly* vexed," or "*i'sooth*"—went the way of all overused words, notes *The Cambridge History of English and American Literature;* they were replaced by less punchy (and, it seems, successively more anemic) eighteenth-century forms such as *vastly* and *prodigiously.*

When intensifiers lack force, they are sometimes propped up by italics—"she was *very* important, *very* rich"—or, in speech, by volume and theatrical pauses: "She was a [pause] *WONDERFULLY* [pause] special person." But when used repeatedly, such props become so weak that they de-intensify; they become gnat-like and annoying. As suggested in Chapter 6, *wonderfully* and other *-ly* adverbs too worn to intensify effectively are best used in sarcastic figures of speech such as paradoxes and oxymorons: *She was wonderfully dismal.*

So again, writers are advised to learn words whose meanings incorporate the sense of *very* or *really* and the like. This is good advice; writers must build forceful vocabularies. But how rigorously should one replace stock intensifiers with these power words? Should one annihilate all common intensifiers, or strike some sort of balance?

Force / Stimulation by Any Means

INTENSIFIERS IN THE BLOOD

In *The Elements of Style,* Strunk and White considered such intensifiers as *very* and *pretty* to be "the leeches that infest the pond of prose, sucking the blood of words." Avoid their use, they ruled.

I would say avoid *unrelenting* use, but do not throw out the pond water with the leeches. Well, maybe I wouldn't say that. I would say this: Intensifiers run in the blood of natural speech; they might be seen, if not as red cells, then as the leukocytes that help defend against fancy-schmancy invaders. Sometimes replacing stock intensifiers with erudite vocabulary can sound labored or arcane—too writerly. "If it sounds like writing, I rewrite it," Elmore Leonard once advised. You may not want to lose the honesty and gestural quality of ordinary speech. So instead of writing *She sensed something very bad—very bad, indeed,* should you write, *She sensed something execrable?* In most contexts, probably not. Save power vocabulary for when its distinctive force is needed—which will be often enough—or for when a narrator's voice demands it. Streams of high-performance words can burden the reader, clot the flow.

Stock intensifiers are so much a part of the English idiom that our prose feels uncomfortable without them. They may do little intensifying, as the rhetoricians say, yet they are part of the background rhythms of our language, the anticipated beats of narration. Speakers often deliver them with musical inflection—"He's *REALLY* hot"—which is welcome relief amidst the monotone of average American speech.

To some degree, an intensifier acts as a signal: it announces that the word following it is worn out, and that it should be understood as inadequate. For example, in the phrase *an utterly beautiful night,* the author is saying, "Look, I *mean* something beyond beautiful, even if I don't have the precise word; try to imagine it."

We've been sending such messages forever—straining like shot-putters for some extra distance, because most words are inadequate, and power-packed modifiers do not leap to the average tongue.

A 2004 research study[1] suggests the extent to which intensifiers are embedded in colloquial speech. Researchers counted 1,886 uses of intensifiers in eight years' worth of episodes of the sitcom *Friends.* Leading the pack was *so,* accounting for 45 percent of the total uses, followed by *really* (25 percent) and *very* (15 percent). (These findings paralleled those of an earlier study of speakers in northeastern England. In that study, the overall rate of intensification was the same, as were the three most-used intensifiers, though they were used with differing frequency: *very* was the most common, followed by *really* and *so.*) The 2004 study also posited that it was female speakers who initiated the rise of *so* as the great American intensifier (see sidebar, "The So-Special Case of *so,*" below).

Just because intensifiers course through informal speech, must we also use them in journalism and literature? Not necessarily—but we certainly *can* use them in situations where they feel natural, or communicate a particular tone. At the very least, we should not hamstring our writing styles trying to replace each intensifier with a more powerful locution.

Scan any respectable publication and you'll find intensifiers that no editor saw fit to slash, albeit some of them in quoted remarks. ("It's very amazing," said Boston Red Sox manager Terry Francona of the team's epic 2004 season.) In the space of just two weeks, as I was writing this chapter, 576 *reallys* and 243 *actuallys*

---

[1]Sali Tagliamonte and Chris Roberts. "So Weird; So Cool; So Innovative: The Use of Intensifiers in the Television Series *Friends*" (paper presented at a meeting of the American Dialect Society, Boston, Mass., 2004).

Force / Stimulation by Any Means

appeared in the *Washington Post.* And in literature? Shakespeare applied *very* and *truly* to legions of modifiers. Or take a novel like Dave Eggers' *A Heartbreaking Work of Staggering Genius:* Not only is it staggeringly good, but its much-praised "full-throttle" style embraces stock intensifiers throughout, as in "an extremely happening walk," "you were so not dressed fine," "nothing really is all that real anymore," and "This is bad. This is so bad. This is unbelievably bad. This is so unbelievably bad."

Even in poetry, where stock anything is usually fatal, the colloquial qualities of intensifiers can be woven into themes—though the weaving is best left to such masters of the conversational voice as Billy Collins. In his "Workshop," for example—a poem that critiques itself, poetry-workshop-style—he describes his poet's voice as "very casual, very blue jeans."

THE SO-SPECIAL CASE OF *SO*

The easily uttered *so* is a venerable English word; *swa,* an early form of it, predates *Beowulf.* Few of *so*'s thirty-odd contemporary meanings present usage problems. But *so* the intensifier, in spite of at least 1,600 years' use, has a way of associating itself with annoying speech habits and winding up on people's hit lists.

E. B. White was among those who targeted the usage for extinction. "Avoid, in writing," he decreed in *The Elements of Style,* "the use of *so* as an intensifier: 'so good'; 'so warm'; 'so delightful.' " Never mind that White used it in his own writings—for example, in his lovely essay, "Once More to the Lake," in which he describes a school of minnows "so clear and sharp in the sunlight."

[124] In the 1970s, not long after White issued his decree, editor Harry G. Nickels also attacked the wee intensifier, targeting what he called "the effect of

girlish gushing" created by a stressed *so*. He urged "the agents of Women's Liberation and Gay Liberation" to cure themselves of the habit of using such expressions as "Her dress was so skimpy."

But *so*, the little intensifier that could, keeps chugging along, finding its way into our language. Such recommended intensifiers as *indeed* or *extremely* stand little chance against the well-oiled, sibilant *so*. In fact, *so*'s reach now extends far beyond the modification of mere adverbs and adjectives; it has become an intensifier of nouns, noun phrases, and just about any part of speech imaginable: *so now; so President Bush; so last year; so dot-com; so "I'm-in-charge-here-and-what-I-say-goes."*

Ever-intense young language users have stretched the *so* envelope to create a potent negative intensifier: "You are so *not* my parents anymore!" But although this locution has embedded itself in our vernaculars, it remains so not standard English.

Use of the intensive *so* itself, however, can be judged case by case. After an audience with Pope John Paul II, a New York psychiatrist remarked that His Holiness "is so single-mindedly focused." Was this not intensifying an intensifier of His Intensity? Maybe. But, hey—for this subject, there are dispensations.

WHEN NOT TO USE INTENSIFIERS

Unless excessive, then, intensifiers usually do no harm, and even have their places—they "ease a phrase now and then," as writing mentor Sheridan Baker allowed. But there are instances when avoiding them is the prudent choice. Most irritating are intensifiers that, instead of boosting the effects of other words, call negative attention to themselves. They do so when they are

- fading out of vogue (*mondo, mega, majorly, hella, fer sure*);
- absurdly redundant (extremely unique, very sublime, *completely* perfect);

[125]

- epidemic, especially among teens (*totally, basically, incredibly, amazingly, unbelievably*);
- repeated and stacked (*really, really, actually* sincere);
- clichéd (*deeply* disturbing; *basically* sound); or
- shoehorned from vernacular into formal usage (*Real Simple* magazine).

Fussy language users (including fussy fictional characters) might also refrain from pairing *very* with verb-based words, unless the pairings are already idiomatic. Thus, the idiomatic *very depressed* is all right, but the rarer *very decimated* should be refined to *very much decimated.* And if I had to explain why, I'd be very much discomfited.

Then again, if you want to get playful in some frisky context, dare to use *very* to intensify a verb: *She was very hungry and, dude, she very ate."* You will have intensified a verb *big-time,* and so what if some grammarian *quite* loses his lunch?

SEVENTEEN

OPENING WORDS:
THE GLORIOUS PORTAL

I promise that something will stimulate you if you continue reading.

Do your opening sentences make that promise? Do they vow to scratch the reader's eternal itch for sensation? How else to keep readers from the suck of wall-sized entertainment monitors? How else to compete with the legions of adept, promise-making writers?

One hears the terms *hook* and *benefit* in connection with openings; but stimulation—perhaps another way of saying "bite"—is what wins the day. To say you will stimulate today's already-bombarded readers seems a cocky promise; but most of what bombards them is numbingly generic. Compelling words, on the other hand, still have the power to seize the reader's imagination, which is always eager to follow hints and implications down the rabbit hole into new realms of feeling.

Fiction, by its very nature, promises to transport readers to imaginative realms. Good openings are a bonus, but less critical than what develops after them. Even the frenetic reader acknowledges, with a twitch, that it may take some time for fictional landscapes to materialize. It is nonfiction that needs the glorious portal: a gateway that declares, "something will stimulate you if you continue reading."

[127]

Force / Stimulation by Any Means

It may seem odd that people have to be induced to read truth, which is what nonfiction purports to be. But truth carries no inherent promises of stimulation—not even truth presented as art. ("In art, truth that is boring is not art," said writer Isaac Bashevis Singer.) Some of the most stupefying content in the cosmos can be classified as truth, as can some of the most soul-stirring. "I promise that *my* truth will stir the pants off your soul," is the message readers of nonfiction want to hear from you—and they want to hear it within the first few sentences.

Truth has another problem: People feel they have heard most of it, five times over. "Tell me something I don't know," says the reader. "Or tell me something I know in a way that stimulates me—starting now!"

Oh, what cruel burdens for an opening paragraph or two! No wonder some writers feel they have to load every hooking device, pyrotechnical locution, and winking charm into their openings. You know the style:

> There are worse spots to wait for Bill Murray than the Vince Lombardi Rest Area on the New Jersey Turnpike. Sure, the place smells like p—s, and feels like a peep-show booth, but it's got the Jersey-rest-stop grand slam: A TCBY, a Nathan's Famous, a Burger King, *and* a Cinnabon. (—Scott Raab, *Esquire*)

A promise of gonzo-type stimulation to be sure; but one more element and it might overflow, sort of like a rest stop trash barrel.

WHAT'S IN A PROMISE

An opening might promise shock, surprise, inspiration, or amusement; or self-improvement and other transformations; or aesthetic pleasure, material gain, enlightenment, titillation, fright, even sorrow. Anything that makes the juices flow.

Promises can be explicit: *Young Angela's story of pain and courage will touch every heart.* The implicit approach is generally more effective, however. As they say in the writing game, let the reader make the connection between stimulus and sensation: *Angela, age 11, has never left her room.*

The openings we will cite here are from various eras and types of nonfiction. Not only have they stood the test of time, but they also demonstrate the virtues of today's best beginnings: As promises, they are uncomplicated, convincing, and true to what's delivered; and as creative writing, they employ such elements of style as:

- Symbolism: small details suggesting grand meanings
- Understatement: less implying more
- Contrast: tension between two or more elements
- Foreboding: hints of trouble ahead
- Force: sensual imagery, powerful verbs
- Intimacy: establishment of a connection between narrator and reader

Anne Frank opened her diary with the words, "I hope I will be able to confide everything to you, as I have never been able to confide in anyone." For Anne's story, that simple promise, styled with intimacy, is an opening that defies improvement.

WRITING THE OPENING: HOW SOON, HOW MUCH

How writers get going on openings may depend on their personalities. Some authors have to fashion a polished opening before they begin the rest of the story. Their opening sets a tone and direction. It inspires them to live up to a beautifully articulated promise. It is money in the bank. And it is compulsive, because such writers know they will only pick at the opening later, maybe rewrite it entirely. Other authors, perhaps more rational, slap down any opening to get the story rolling, then come back to craft it according to what follows. They might find that a buried anecdote, even their punchy conclusion, contains the nugget of the ideal opening. Either approach can work, but the compulsive types suffer the usual anguish.

We say the opening promise has to be delivered in a few sentences; how few depends mainly on the length of the work. Readers of a newspaper or magazine piece, already stimulated by headlines, subheads, and graphic enticements, expect a fast, focused entry—maybe three or four sentences at most: "Norman Mailer's new book bears all the signs—all the watermarks, all the heraldry—of a writer faced with an alimony bill of $500,000." (Martin Amis, *The Observer,* 1982) Readers may be more patient with book and chapter openings, but within a half page or so they should be convinced that soul or synapse will be jostled at some point down the line.

Sometimes a slow, percolating beginning seems the only way to launch a complex piece; but slow is hazardous in an age of manic impatience. Prolonged openings are mainly an indulgence of brand-name authors. However, they sometimes work as a sampling of things to come, like a musical overture, delivering both promise and stimulation. For example, Mark Twain's opening to *Life on the Mississippi* is a 238-word paragraph that winds its way through the river's awesome statistics, promising a larger-than-life tale while making the reader a little smarter. And when Tom Wolfe opens his *Kandy-Kolored Tangerine-Flake Streamline Baby* by repeating the word *hernia* fifty-seven times to mimic the singsong of a Vegas craps dealer, readers are already having a laugh and anticipating more.

A CERTAIN SOMETHING

Speaking of hernia, in my life as an editor I hefted no few truckloads of nonfiction submissions; and like other editors who have seen every earnest and devious attempt to grab attention in an opening, I tended to appreciate those efforts that seemed effortless and yet had *something* that left a bite mark. What can that something be? One fetching quality is sincerity: a sense that what follows the opening will come from the heart—whether the heart be desolate or overflowing. It worked long ago for St. Augustine, who in the opening of Book III of *The Confessions* revealed the conflicted state of his passions:

> I went to Carthage, where I found myself in the midst of a hissing cauldron of lust. I had not yet fallen in love, but I was in love with the idea of it, and this feeling that something was missing made me despise myself for not being more anxious to satisfy the need. . . . I had no liking for the safe path without pitfalls. (ca. 400)

It is said that Thomas Paine, marching in retreat with George Washington's troops in 1776, scrawled the opening words to *American Crisis* using the head of a drum as a desk. They still resound like a drumbeat:

> These are the times that try men's souls. The summer soldier and the sunshine patriot will, in this crisis, shrink from the ser-

vice of their country; but he that stands it *now,* deserves the love and thanks of man and woman. (1776)

CONTEXT COUNTS

Opening words can release a torrent of feelings when an audience, owing to cultural or historical events, is poised to react to them. The writer's job is to find expression for readers' pent-up sensibilities. Betty Friedan's *The Feminine Mystique* touched tens of millions with its opening:

> The problem lay buried, unspoken, for many years in the minds of American women. It was a strange stirring, a sense of dissatisfaction, a yearning that women suffered in the middle of the twentieth century in the United States. . . . the silent question—"Is this all?" (1963)

In *Roots,* Alex Haley shared his triumphant genealogical odyssey with multitudes of other African-Americans who felt detached from their ancestral histories. The book's vigorous opening brought his triumph to life:

> Early in the spring of 1750, in the village of Juffure, four days upriver from the coast of The Gambia, West Africa, a manchild was born to Omoro and Binta Kinte. Forcing forth from Binta's strong young body, he was as black as she was, flecked and slippery with Binta's blood, and he was bawling. (1976)

TYPES OF—HOW YOU SAY?—"LEADS"

Journalists call the opening lines of their stories "leads" (pronounced *leeds,* sometimes spelled *ledes*), a term so newsroomy it sports a fedora and sleeve garters. We might as well start using it here—even applying it, as journalists do, to openings in literature.

Every so often someone tries to catalog all the many types of leads. Editor Robert L. Baker once defined seventeen types, including the standard news summary (which answers the questions "who?", "what?", "where?", and "when?") and the "hybrid," or mix of types. Actually, inventive writers have devised dozens of approaches, but much of their work begins with one of six types of openings identified by Baker:

- someone's remark—a quotation;
- an intriguing or amusing question;
- a striking or startling statement;
- descriptive stage-setting;
- storytelling narrative; or
- a one-line attention getter called a "capsule."

Using the capsule lead followed by taut narratives in *The Miami Herald,* crime reporter and mystery writer Edna Buchanan created such classic openings as this one from 1985:

> **Gary Robinson died hungry.**
> **He wanted fried chicken, the three-piece box for $2.19.**

The story goes on to reveal how the protagonist pushes his way through the line at a fast-food joint, punches the counter girl because the supply of chicken has run out, and is shot three times by a security guard.

The stage-setter is a slower type of lead. Tipped off to a story's subject by headlines or titles, readers know the staging will be relevant and they enjoy the drama—but only for a few paragraphs before they start stamping for action. To set the stage for their Pulitzer Prize–winning series on gene therapy, the *Chicago Tri-*

[133]

Force / Stimulation by Any Means

bune's Jeff Lyon and Peter Gomer panned the bedroom of a young girl suffering from an immune system deficiency:

> Entering Allison Ashcraft's bedroom you get the feeling that you are being watched. Stuffed animals are everywhere. More than 200 of them fix visitors with a glassy stare from all corners of the room. Girlish excess? No, good parental psychology. Each button-eyed, felt-tongued rabbit, tiger, and bear represents a time in the last five years that doctors have had to draw Allison's blood. (1986)

Sports writers like to set stages to the point of cliché, perhaps ever since 1924, when Notre Dame beat Army's football team and Grantland Rice immortalized four players in this lead for the *New York Herald-Tribune:*

> Outlined against a blue-gray October sky, the Four Horsemen rode again. In dramatic lore they are known as Famine, Pestilence, Destruction and Death. These are only aliases. Their real names are Stuhldreher, Miller, Crowley and Layden.

In the same tradition but without cliché, John Updike began his *New Yorker* adieu to Ted Williams with this stage-setter:

> Fenway Park, in Boston, is a lyric little bandbox of a ball park. Everything is painted green and seems in curiously sharp focus, like the inside of an old-fashioned, peeping-type Easter egg. (*The New Yorker,* 1960)

The good narrative lead gets right to the action—setting the stage, if necessary, as it goes along. If vicarious thrills are to come, they can start coming in the lead itself:

[134]

We were all strapped into the seats of the Chinook, fifty of us, and something was hitting it from the outside with an enormous hammer . . . making it dip and turn in a horrible out-of-control motion that took me in the stomach.

(—Michael Herr, "Illumination Rounds," *Dispatches,* 1977)

STRIKING TO THE QUICK

The striking-statement type of lead can pierce even the thickest armor of reader resistance. Strike directly at a reader's fears, sacred cows, or funny bone, and you'll get attention.

Opening a chapter of *Silent Spring,* Rachel Carson went for the fear membrane:

For the first time in the history of the world, every human being is now subjected to contact with dangerous chemicals, from the moment of conception until death. (1962)

Among author William Zinsser's favorite leads is one of his own, the droll but unsettling opening to "Block that Chicken-furter," from a 1969 issue of *Life* magazine: "I've often wondered what goes into a hot dog. Now I know and I wish I didn't."

Whatever its slant, the striking statement should be concise and, ideally, involve the reader. In 1990, Diane Ackerman drew readers into the "Vision" chapter of *A Natural History of the Senses* with this twist on self-image: "Look in the mirror. The face that pins you with its double gaze reveals a chastening secret: You are looking into a predator's eyes." Here, Ackerman uses the "direct" (or second-person) approach to engage the reader's self-interest. A first-person approach can be equally engaging, provided that nothing distracts the reader from identifying with the "I" character. "I come to celebrate celery," wrote Dorothy Kallins as her

[135]

Force / Stimulation by Any Means

lead to "Crunch" (*Saveur*, 2001)—and we can already taste what's coming.

OVERWORKED OPENINGS

"A good lead overcomes the inertia that sits on a reader's mind like a lump of clay." This is an example of the "quotation lead"—and one that makes a good point. But as a type of lead, the quotation is becoming shopworn—thanks partly to a million speech openings.

In profiles and interviews, however, where the subject's words are paramount and usually fresh, the quotation still rules:

> "A good thread," said the Mahatma, "is a thing of beauty and a joy forever."
>
> With the fingers of one hand he maintained the proper delicate tension on the cotton thread he was spinning. With the other hand he turned the small, flat charkha—spinning wheel—at his side on the white mattress. (—Price Day, *Baltimore Sun*, 1948)

Just as the quotation lead worked in this Pulitzer Prize–winning interview with Gandhi, it can work in today's profiles if brief and pointed.

But some devices that once put a literary gloss on works of nonfiction are today seeming rather weather-beaten. Gandhi spinning thread, for example, is one of those detailed close-ups meant to contrast with earthshaking events—in this case with rioting and social upheaval in India. Related clichés include the "calm before the storm" opening, or what William Zinsser once called "the button-nosed-boy" approach: the paper boy completing his route before the sleepy town explodes.

Don't shy away from literary devices in your leads—or even from cinematic pans and zooms. But try to resist clichéd types as rigorously as you avoid long lists, asides, and complicated background details. Be original, and watch that lump of clay melt away.

THE PERSONAL TOUCH

In first-person narratives—memoirs, autobiographies, accounts of journeys—many of the best openings are invitational rather than startling. They imply, "Here is a person you want to spend time with." Few readers want to hang with a bloviating show-off; but openings that suggest some exceptional personality trait of the narrator promise stimulating company. Naturally, this suggestion must be true to the character of the whole work.

Readers love setting off on physical or spiritual journeys with keen-eyed companions. Paul Theroux portrays himself as an intolerant loner in his travel adventures, yet readers want to come along to share his observations, both mean-spirited and soulful. In his opening to *The Great Railway Bazaar,* he hints that the soulful side is on board:

> Ever since childhood, when I lived within earshot of the Boston and Maine, I have seldom heard a train go by and not wished I was on it. Those whistles sing bewitchment: railways are irresistible bazaars, snaking along perfectly level no matter what the landscape, improving your mood with speed, and never upsetting your drink. (1975)

In your own first-person openings, you may want to introduce a touch of your wit or special savvy; your literary flair, nuttiness, perceptiveness—even wickedness. Alice Roosevelt Longworth's conversational opener is legend: "If you can't say something good about someone, sit right here by me." Your opening, too, can radio a signal to kindred souls.

What do you think drew a million-plus readers into a little book about punctuation with the puzzling title *Eats, Shoots &*

Force / Stimulation by Any Means

Leaves? Partly it was author Lynne Truss's ability to issue a mating call with her opening sentences:

> Either this will ring bells for you or it won't. A printed banner has appeared on the concourse of a petrol station near to where I live. "Come inside," it says, "for CD's, VIDEO's, DVD's, and BOOK's."
>
> If this satanic sprinkling of redundant apostrophes causes no little gasp of horror or quickening of the pulse, you should probably put down this book at once.

LITERARY OPENINGS

Leads in the literary style, prone to excess or pretension, may be the trickiest to pull off. But good writing, when it prevails, burnishes a lead that already has something to say. For example, thousands of war reports have captured readers by virtue of their timeliness, their immediate relevance. Those that endure, however, tend to have a literary touch. Who but Ernest Hemingway could have written this lead to a Spanish Civil War dispatch?

> The window of the hotel is open and, as you lie in bed, you hear the firing in the front line seventeen blocks away. There is rifle fire all night long. The rifles go tacrong, capong, craang, tacrong, and then a machine gun opens up. . . . You lie and listen to it, and it is a great thing to be in bed with your feet stretched out gradually warming the cold foot of the bed and not out there. (NANA dispatch, 1937)

Science writers—nature writers in particular—often favor the literary approach, so rhapsodic are they about their subjects.

While the gushiest leads need capping, a deft writer like Richard Selzer (*Mortal Lessons*) promises art as well as fact:

> I sing of skin, layered as fine as baklava, whose colors shame the dawn, at once the scabbard upon which is writ our only signature, and the instrument by which we are thrilled, protected, and kept constant in our natural place. Here is each man bagged and trussed in perfect amiability. (1976)

LEADS FOR LAUGHS

The successful comedic lead, one that promises sustained mirth, must obey two cardinal rules: Be fast, and be funny. The supreme master of this form is humorist Dave Barry, who has quickly pried laughs from his readers in thousands of openings. Along the way, in a column called "Socket to Them," he mocked the popular-science lead:

> Today's scientific question is, What in the world is electricity? And where does it go after it leaves the toaster? Here is a simple experiment that will teach you an important electrical lesson: On a cool, dry day, scuff your feet along the carpet, then reach your hand into a friend's mouth and touch one of his dental fillings. (—*Bad Habits*, 1985)

So there you are. And here's a related experiment for writers. Have a friend or younger sibling poke a finger between your teeth. Bite down. Observe the reaction. Is there stimulation? Is attention being paid? Aha—could it be a paradigm?

Now, releasing the finger, go write your lead.

Force / Stimulation by Any Means

EIGHTEEN

CLOSINGS: THE THREE-POINT LANDING

You are piloting a jumbo jetliner—just another of your cocky gestures—and somehow you have managed to take off, maintain a cruising altitude, and cross a continent. At last you are approaching the destination airport with your precious cargo intact. One problem: You have no idea how to get this baby down.

Ever get that feeling with an ambitious piece of writing, especially in nonfiction? You've achieved liftoff against all odds, navigated past every hazard. But now you're stuck in mid-air.

As writers, we naturally focus on beginning a work and developing it, on all the challenges of getting and holding attention. Along the way we don't think much about endings—just that we will write to length and make concluding noises in the last paragraph. But when we get there, feeling the expectations of all those readers invested in the journey, we wish we could touch down as gracefully, as meaningfully, as Apollo 11 did on the moon.

In a nonfiction piece, an ending isn't the end of the world— just the climax to everything you've labored to make affecting and saleable. Endings are last impressions. They are closing numbers, final chords, deal-sealers. They deliver readers to the intended destination, influence what satisfaction each will take away. For the many readers who browse endings or peek ahead to see where their efforts will lead, endings can be invitations—the flip side of powerful openings.

Those who outline their work have an opportunity to think about the closing, perhaps even rough out a concept. For other writers, a landing strategy is worth having in place before take-off—but it needn't involve control towers and runway lights. The idea is simply to end by design rather than default, and any of the following practices will help:

- In your notes, keep track of potentially dramatic closing materials.
- Hold one of your best examples or anecdotes for the closing.
- Allow space for a developed ending.
- Commit to a closing worthy of the piece.
- Avoid the drift toward a clichéd ending.

FLIPPING THE OLD PYRAMID

The art of conclusion is as old as rhetoric, but always amenable to new twists. Many journalists have moved away from the traditional "inverted pyramid" of news writing, in which the most cuttable material appears at the end of a piece (in case it runs long). The New Journalism, with its personal, featurish approach to reporting, encouraged artful closings that editors were expected to spare. Endings now range from the literary to the pontifical, while flip closings à la *Time* magazine find a thousand imitators. (A *Time* original: "Ken and Ric Burns have managed to sing America. If only they wouldn't sing it to sleep.")

Better such flippancy, however, than the soporific endings favored in corporate and professional literature. In one recent article, the author could have pulled at least two living, breathing endings from the text's middle mass, but instead concluded with this: "Vision, creativity, and initiative are the main ingredients of a successful partnership, leading professionals along innovative paths to collective development." Can you stand the excitement? No resonance, no concretion, no twist. The writer seems to have followed the classic "tell-'em" formula popular among luncheon speakers: "Tell 'em what you're gonna say, then say it, then tell 'em what you just said." The formula encourages summation endings, often the most abstracted and least interesting type. In writing, the more creative (if demanding) formula would be: "Promise to stimulate 'em, stimulate 'em, and leave 'em stimulated." Not that we want to overstimulate a bunch of *'ems* wolfing their lunch; but for our readers, the best *digestif* might be a concluding poke in the labonza.

THE HEN THAT LAYS THE GOLDEN ENDINGS

A writer can arrive at the closing point of a story with all the space and commitment necessary for a brilliant ending, but feeling like a sucked-out egg when it comes to ideas. Sometimes the quickest remedy is to reach into the basket of conventional closings, choosing one of several models. Because such models are patterned on familiar usages, they can easily steer one toward cliché; but they can also inspire imaginative and even unconventional variations. It's all in the execution, as they say.

Writers' guides often treat types of endings, but tend to quote long and tedious passages to illustrate them in context. Here, in the interest of brevity, I've composed eight contemporary endings to an already well-known business story—that of a young entrepreneur named Jack who trades the family cow for a few magic beans, climbs a beanstalk, and winds up a billionaire.

SOME CONVENTIONAL MODELS FOR ENDINGS

Closed circle, or "bookend." A model in which the ending echoes or completes the opening: Yes, *"once upon a time there was a poor widow with an only son named Jack." Now it's poor Jack who faces time—for theft and tax fraud—in a kingdom where beans don't count.*

Judgment. In this model, used mainly in opinion pieces, an explicit closing pronouncement should add something—if only in style—to judgments made earlier in the text: *Jack's wealth was dirty from the start, his fowl ill-gotten; but the cry of 'foul!' was nowhere to be heard."*

Implication. Implicit judgments characterize such endings. Often they contain rhetorical questions: *True, the giant made some bad choices. He ate Englishmen. He abused his wife. But Jack made choices, too. Should he not have to live with them?*

Legacy. These closings offer advice to the reader: *Jack had it all: golden eggs, bags of treasure, talking harp. But he forgot one thing: The higher you climb up a beanstalk, the more the world sees your worst end. Maybe some of us should just stay grounded.*

Anecdote or vignette. The little closing stories used in this model are on-message or take an ironic twist: *Recently I ran across the very peddler who traded the magic beans to Jack. Now struggling in the commodities market, he bears rueful memories of the big one that got away. "And here's the worst part," he laments. "That cow was a lemon!"*

Call to action. Such endings often work better in a sidebar than in the main text of a piece: *With his derring-do, Jack has given untold*

Force / Stimulation by Any Means

pleasure to generations of story-lovers. Today he asks only one thing: Help in achieving justice. Contributions to the Beanstalk Legal Defense Fund may be sent to . . .

Revelation. Here, one provides telling details that have been (reasonably) withheld. An author comment may be added: *As it turns out, Jack's mother was anything but poor; tax records reveal vacation properties in the Swiss Alps. Would her telling Jack have made a difference? Probably not. When magic rules, we are all captives of its spell.*

Quotation. Endings of this type are sometimes dramatized—for example: *The giant's widow paused in her herb garden to reflect on the one-time thief who slew her husband. "As far as Jack goes—no hard feelings. Look, I was married to a monster, now I'm free." She bent to pinch off a basil leaf, then looked up. "I don't care about the hen. Jack gave me my life back. He deserves a break."*

TOP CLICHÉS

You can see how the above models flirt with some of the most clichéd endings in popular media—broadcast news in particular. One has to be inventive with them, but avoiding such models altogether may be impossible and even unwise; some are simply apt forms of punctuation for ongoing news. Even a touch of pumped-up rhetoric is acceptable in closings, so time-honored is the big finish. But when endings yield to some of the punchless clichés that follow (in italics), a rest and a rewrite might be in order:

- With a team of lawyers, young Jack may yet beat the charges. *But one thing is certain:* There'll be no more giant-killing in this lad's future.

- Are the beanstalk seeds a hoax, or will USDA studies turn genetic secrets into a supercrop? *Stay tuned.*
- The case could turn on whether the Poor Widow mastermined Jack's capitalization schemes. But for now, *the jury is still out.*
- Although Jack Enterprises, Ltd., has experienced fiduciary issues, aggressive refocusing assures that the company *is well positioned for the future.*

Specialized forms of media have their own clichéd closings, such as this persistent one in the popular health media: *Before trying any new therapy, be sure to discuss it first with your physician.* (As if!) One way to beat such clichés is with well-chosen quotations, which are unique and personal and relieve the monotony of the author's voice. For example, a recent report on ten newly discovered planets closed with this quotation from an astronomer: "Gosh, when you look at the next sun out, it's got planets, too . . . suggesting that planets are as common as cheap hotels."

LANDING BY THE RULES

The usual rules of forceful writing apply to endings, too. Make them fresh, concrete, and sincere. Use evocative language. Less can be more. Show, don't tell—and so on. Here's a few more "do's" and "do not's" culled from several sources, including *Leads and Conclusions* by Marshall J. Cook, and *On Writing Well* by William Zinsser:

Do Not
- change an article's tone at the end;
- add a gratuitous tag such as "indeed" to a quote;

[145]

- suddenly introduce new or irrelevant ideas;
- drag endings out unnecessarily;
- make early concluding sounds ("Finally, let us review . . . ," etc.); or
- take the last word away from interviewees.

Do
- put ringing quotes aside for endings;
- stop when it feels right to stop;
- create a clear sense of completion;
- leave room for reader reflection;
- offer surprises that, in retrospect, make sense;
- get personal, as in "I want you to remember this one thing . . .";
- leave readers with a feeling of uplift or insight—of gain.

Now how do I bring this baby down? For that purpose, I have sneakily set aside a piece of advice from my readings. Not only is it an inspirational quote, but it implies that writers can blame someone else for lousy endings. And what could be more satisfying than that?

[Make] your conclusions so good, so integral to their stories, [that] even the most insensitive scissor-wielding, delete-punching editor should know enough to leave them alone."

(—Marshall J. Cook)

Form

LIFE BETWEEN THE MARKS

NINETEEN

THE JOYS OF HYPER-HYPHENATION

The *oh-my-God-the-pain* poetry. The *everyone-lets-you-down-in-the-end* novellas. . . . From my student days in the Iowa Writers Workshop I can still recall the extended, hyphenated modifiers we used in critiquing each other's literary attempts. We didn't know the device's name back then, only that it helped us mock writers of those *so-great-because-it-happened-to-me* short stories.

It seemed we could lasso any idea, including our own high concepts, with such hyphenated strings as *A love-conquers-all dreamer in a cesspool-of-the-cosmos trailer park.* Of course as our writing matured (ahem), we came to use such modifiers with discretion, realizing how quickly they can grow tedious.

Among rhetoricians the hyper-modified form has come to be known as a "Teutonicism," or the easier-to-say "Germanism," from the Germanic pattern of stacking modifiers in front of the thing modified. In front-loaded German syntax, an English phrase like *turkey stuffed with breading and savory spices* becomes *with breading and savory spices stuffed turkey.* Front-loading a compound modifier in English and stringing it together with hyphens does more than change word order: It can make for quirky, whimsical expression, as well as jargon (*mission-critical implementation*) and campy excess. How excessive is the excess? In a recent send-up of reality shows, a National Public Radio commentator referred to an "oh-my-God-I-can't-believe-you-just-did-that-especially-in-light-of-what-you-said-at-the-beach-house-yesterday cringe."

ANTI-GERMANISM-TYPE GUYS

Energetic, farcical Germanisms are so embedded in contemporary style that we might be hard-put to do without them. But not so long ago among America's language authorities, they were about as welcome as bedbugs. Writing in the 1920s, H. W. Fowler had no use for the form, which he said reflected "the compression characteristic of journalese." In the 1960s, Wilson Follett blamed American advertisers for burdening our nouns with these mixed parts of speech agglutinated by hyphens. Such Germanisms, he charged, substituted contrived adjectives for articulate expression. His bugbears included "easy-to-read books" and "ready-to-bake food."

Rudolph Flesch hailed the creativity of certain hyphenated modifiers. He liked "barefoot-boy-born-in-a-cabin credentials" and "come-as-the-person-you-like-best-or-least parties." But like Fowler, he considered a Germanism such as "the Kennedy-sought tax cut" an ugly device for stuffing extra information into a sentence. *The New Fowler's,* too, suggests restraint when hyphenating becomes "burdensome," as in the phrase "a nuclear-weapon-free world."

Restraint, however, is hardly the hallmark of American writing. In 1965, Tom Wolfe's *The Kandy-Kolored Tangerine-Flake Streamline Baby* helped elevate both journalese and Germanisms into high art. And by 1996, *Wired Style: Principles of English Usage in the Digital Age* was smiling upon "over-the-top writing that relies on a string of hyphenated words."

[149]

HYPHEN-HAPPY LOCUTIONS

Contemporary writers are having fun with stacked-up, hyphenated modifiers (Germanisms)—but their readers? Here are a dozen samples of mixed artistry for you to judge. Perhaps the best ones will inspire your own bold agglutinations. But remember: Overdo it and you may sound like some I'm-just-sitting-here-shooting-out-hyphens-until-an-adjective-comes-to-mind airhead.

"... a Grow-Your-Own-Warts kit." (—J. K. Rowling, *Harry Potter and the Sorcerer's Stone*)

"[Fidelity in marriage is] a storybook device, it's some retro Knights-of-the-Round-Table Camelot-and-chivalry deal." (—Salman Rushdie, *The Ground Beneath Her Feet*)

"I'm not a food person in the let's-go-to-Spruce-I-hear-they-have-a-new-chef way." (—Martha Bayne, *Chicago Reader*)

"[His] teeth-baring Iowa finale was so Ross-Perot-scare-off-the-women-and-horses crazy ..." (—Maureen Dowd, *The New York Times*)

"... and not the Nebraska-Ghost-of-Tom-Joad Springsteen, but the Born-to-Run-Two-Hearts-Are-Better-Than-One-Rosalita-(Won't-You-Come-Out-Tonight) Bruce." (—Dennis Lehane, *Mystic River*)

"... hands-in-flannel-trouser-pockets pose." (—Will Self, *How the Dead Live*)

"... white-person-with-dreadlocks-at-a-liberal-arts-college-thing." (—Jamie Schweser, *The Zine Yearbook*)

"There was 'the drats,' a fists-clenching, double-forearm-drop gesture that Lucille [Ball]'s alter ego, Lucy ... would make.... Just as reliable was ... that curl-the-upper-lip, swivel-the-head 'Eyeeeoooough!' exclamation." (—Steve Daly, *Entertainment Weekly*)

"... pledge-drive-friendly aesthetic." (—James Poniewozik, *Time*)

"...electrons—organized into do-with-me-what-you-will currents and let-me-tell-you-what-I'm-thinking pulses.... alligators-in-the-sewers myth.... the crate-broken-open-at-Kennedy theory of the origin of feral parakeets." (—Adam Gopnik, *The New Yorker*)

SEDUCTIVE CHARMS

The charms of Germanisms seduce writers and readers alike. First of all, they save words and simplify sentence structure. For example, why is a "school of thought" so often preceded by a Germanism, as in *the people-can-bloody-well-decide-for-themselves school of thought?* Answer: Because school would be out by the time one said, "the school of thought in which people are considered to be able to decide bloody well for themselves." Reading an in-flight magazine, I admired how one writer derided, with a single jet-speed Germanism, the "[Stephen] King-is-trashy-fun-but-not-real-literature school of thought." The same derision would later require speech-length efforts at an award ceremony for King.

Also seductive is the sarcastic tone of Germanisms, which often read as if to be spoken with exaggerated finger quotes. The form borrows the cachet of new or existing phrases—idioms, catchphrases, titles—when it turns them into compound adjectives: A *Time* reporter, for example, recently sniped at "overbearing I-am-woman-hear-me-roar vibes." Because any word can appear in a Germanism, a writer's stock of modifiers suddenly encompasses every utterance in the universe—a daunting if empowering notion.

As a form of shorthand with attitude, front-loaded modifiers are naturals for use in conversation, especially among youth. Germanisms lend authenticity to juvenile speech in fiction: *Is this the why-don't-you-grow-up part, Dad?; Did you hear about my so-*

[151]

incredibly-embarrassing-I-wanted-to-die-on-the-spot thing at the dance?
A parent might prefer that the child build a vocabulary and say
something like, *Did you hear about my contretemps?* rather than rely
on relatively mindless and often sloppy Germanisms. But would
it ring true as dialogue? Not in my neighborhood.

Adults, too—including writers—sometimes use the form in a
lazy way, avoiding the struggle for precision. One could say, "He
has that boy-do-I-love-it-when-my-enemies-get-shafted way of
thinking," or, alternatively, "he feels schadenfreude." But sometimes a Germanism, with its theatricality, can be livelier or even
more nuanced than a single term.

Little wonder that, with their appealing energy, Germanisms
turn up in literature and journalism at all levels. Appearing in dialogue as well as narrative, they flourish in X-rated expression,
where stacked-up adjectives lend themselves to name-calling.
Hyphens used to fly like bullets in the old American westerns:
"Why you dad-blamed, no-good, yellow-bellied tub-o-guts!"
And in quoting some modern writers (in genteel company), one
needs one bandoleer of hyphens and one of bleeps: "You're a
skinny-bleep snake motherbleeper nobody-to-nothing piece of
street bleep." (Richard Price, *Clockers*) (bleeps mine)

The fun of strung-out Germanisms lies partly in their frenzy—
the rapid-fire fusillade of words and images aimed at one noun,
pronoun, or adjective: "I'm just the cream-soda-swilling . . . over-
alls-over-candy-colored-latex-mini-kimono . . . don't-bother-me-
till-halftime kind of guy that society has made me." (Mark Leyner,
Et Tu, Babe) But two-or-three-word Germanisms can have their
own charms, including offbeat juxtapositions and plays on meanings: *male-simpatico feminists; click-and-mortar retailers; content-free
reflections.* Today such Germanisms are almost de rigueur in American expression, even if awkward new formations such as *faith-
based charities* cause initial wincing.

SPUNK & BITE

THE RULES

Rule Number One of using Germanisms is to consider the intended mood of your work. Playful? Sober? A touch of the wacky or whimsical may be just the ticket—or a big sore thumb. Germanisms created for effect can be out of place in high-minded prose, while those used for precision or economy seem natural.

When, in *The Human Stain,* Philip Roth writes, "a full-to-the-brimming ready-made East Orange world," it is mainly for economy. Most of his Germanisms are of the "conventional" or "standard" type, meaning they are made up of familiar word combinations (e.g., *ready-made, high-minded, cut-and-dried*). The other type of Germanism is called "nonce" or "improvised" (*tangerine-flake, don't-bother-me-till-halftime*); these Germanisms are invented for specific occasions. The line between the two types may blur, but invented, nonce Germanisms are clearly the more affecting—or obtrusive, depending on the writer's skill and timing.

Rule Number Two is to use multiple-hyphen adjectives sparingly and artfully—as if you needed to be told. But their seductiveness can lead even the forewarned to toss off facile Germanisms rather than dig for the right words. Certain types of subjects—among them looks, attitudes, postures, smiles, tones of voice, and schools of thought—inspire Germanisms so readily that to use one may risk cliché. Consider using a word like *demure,* for example, before spewing out, "She had that I'm-a-shy-girl-of-good-breeding-so-treat-me-with-gentle-respect look in her eyes."

For artful use, we suggest favoring Germanisms that achieve an effect—image, mimicry, euphony, rhythm, disjuncture, tension, tone—and discarding those that merely spell out some adjective's meaning. One needn't press for high-art usages;

something like "a low-center-of-gravity guy," as sportscaster John Madden described a girthy football lineman, is art enough.

Rule Number Three is one of form: Insert a hyphen between all the words of a compound adjective when they act together on the thing modified. *Crystal-ball-toting literati* refers to literati toting crystal balls. But *crystal ball-toting literati,* as one magazine punctuated it, depicts literati made of crystal who are toting balls. Maybe the writer saw it that way.

Rule Number Four also deals with form: Be sure to separate compound adjectives with commas when each compound acts independently on what is modified. For example, in the Germanism *a muscle-twitching, wide-eyed specimen,* the word *specimen* is modified in two independent stages; but in *a gluteus-maximus-muscle-twitching specimen,* all the adjectives work as a unit and are linked by hyphens.

And a quick Rule Number Five for all you tightly muscled word-pushers: Do not use hyphens after *-ly* adverbs.

But now we are entering a grammar-is-taking-all-the-fun-out-of-this-chapter area. You get the idea. Be inventive, but stop when you feel you're hyper-hyphenating to the point of passing out.

TWENTY

A LICENSE. TO FRAGMENT.
SENTENCES.

You. Were warned. Against the sentence fragment. The clipped sentence. Way back in composition class. Sentence fragment. Sound familiar? A quasi-statement beginning with a capital, ending with closing punctuation. But lacking a verb. Or subject. Sometimes both. Like these would-be sentences. Which are mere fragments.

Sentence fragments. Incorrect! Never to be used. Except for effect. And only by copywriters, journalists, and literary authors. Not you.

Okay, *hold it.* Can we bring out the verbs and subjects for a minute? Where were we? Oh, yes: At one time you might have learned that stylish writers were allowed to use fragments, but not you; not you the lowly student. Fragments were not for you.

Until now! Because now you are one of those stylish writers. Writer 007: You have a license to fragment. And from time to time, no matter what you are writing—hot news, features, fiction, drama, ad copy—you will fire off the occasional sentence fragment. You will do so because

- fragments are a natural and common form of speech, whether in narration or dialogue;

- they mimic thought snippets;
- they dispense with obvious or repetitious verbiage, such as "*there is*";
- they provide refreshing variations of rhythm and tone within paragraphs; and
- they help writers create special moods, from dreamy to manic.

But you'll want to mind these pitfalls:

- overuse of fragments, rendering them monotonous, ludicrous, and ultimately unbearable;
- worn-out uses—as for example, in hard-boiled narrative: *That doll. A knockout. A killer. Especially with that gat. Aimed at my eyeballs.;*
- lazy uses, where complete sentences would deliver greater force or elegance (see sidebar, "Fragmenting the Great Whale," below).

LOW-MILEAGE FRAGMENTS

Most fragments piggyback on the action of the sentences preceding them, adding some modifying detail or reinforcing imagery: *The vacuum sucked the alien through the porthole. Tentacles first, egg sac last. Into the grip of space. Black. Airless. Lethal.* But the ride can go only so far. Even with the drama provided by full-stop pauses, fragments soon run out of energy. The narrative flow needs a recharge; namely, the power of verbs driving subjects.

Knowing this, most writers go easy on the fragments. Only for special effect do they launch a parade of them. Philip Roth, for example, uses a series of fragments in *The Human Stain* to sketch a woman's thoughts as she tries to sort out her motivations:

> Ambition. Adventure. Glamour. The glamour of going to America. The superiority. The superiority of leaving. Left for the pleasure of one day coming home, having done it, of returning home triumphant.

Poets, with their dispensation from the rules of crafting sentences, sometimes string fragments into whole verses or even poems. Maestros like Canadian poet Anne Carson can pull it off. Many beginners merely pile on single-image fragments until a point is forced: *Her tin of single earrings. / Drawers of pills. / Threadbare wigs. / A girdle, decades old.* But the pile-ups are essentially lists until sentences give them context and direction.

Likewise among prose stylists: the fragments tend to be organized by full sentences. Joan Didion, everyone's favorite representative of the clipped style, uses staccato fragments to underscore tense moods and to evoke the bursts and repetitions of interior monologue. Often in her work, a brief fragment constitutes a whole paragraph. But everything rises out of the mother sentences:

> *There was no doubt we were dealing with forces that*
> *might or might not include predictable elements.*
> *Elements beyond our control.*
> *No doubt, no argument at all.*
> *And yet.*
> *Still.*
> (—*The Last Thing He Wanted*) (italics hers)

FRAGMENTING THE GREAT WHALE

Sound bites, instant messaging, coded vernaculars: Are we moving toward fragmented expression in general, toward a language of clipped sentences and key words? Compared with the prolix, serpentine styles of the nineteenth century, our prose does seem headed that way.

Perhaps fragments put a hop in our writing, help it compete with today's frenetic media. But if laziness were to draw us away from subject-verb constructions, with their rhythms and emphases, we would risk losing the narrative grace, eloquence, and clarity that has always engaged readers. Imagine if Herman Melville's *Moby Dick* had begun as follows. How long before a reader would have jumped ship, whale or no whale?

> Ishmael the name. Years ago, little money in my purse. Or no money. Nothing to interest me on shore. Nothing particular. A thought: sail about a little. A view of the world. The watery part. No more spleen. Regulate the circulation. The symptoms? Grim about the mouth. November in my soul. Damp. Drizzly. High time for some sea. My pistol and ball. Same with all men. Almost all. Same feelings. Toward the ocean. Nearly.

And now, swim among the refreshing verbs in Melville's original opening lines:

> Call me Ishmael. Some years ago—never mind how long precisely— having little or no money in my purse, and nothing particular to interest me on shore, I thought I would sail about a little and see the watery part of the world. It is a way I have of driving off the spleen, and regulating the circulation. Whenever I find myself growing grim about the mouth; whenever it is a damp, drizzly November in my soul; . . . then, I account it high time to get to sea as soon as I can. This is my substitute for pistol and ball. . . . If they but knew it, almost all men in their degree,

some time or other, cherish very nearly the same feelings towards the ocean with me.

OLD FRAGMENTS & NEW

Today's cell phone addicts, E-mailers, and text messagers embrace sentence fragments as if they'd invented them. And perhaps they—we—have done just that, reinventing a rhetorical device as a conversational code:

> *Yo, word?*
> *Hey. Same old.*
> *Me 2.*
> *Kinda wired L8tly.*
> *Starbucks much?*
> *Yeah. Really.*

But surely we *sapiens* grunted fragments long before we formed sentences, and we've probably never stopped. Had our fragmenting skills flagged, the telegraph would have revived them—*DIVORCING YOU. STOP.*—not to mention the clipped utterances of Jack Webb on TV's *Dragnet* in the 1950s: "Just the truth, ma'am." In literature, fragments appeared in the Bible and other venerable texts, eventually coming to serve an aesthetic purpose in such classics as Charles Dickens's *Bleak House:*

> **London. Michaelmas term lately over, and the Lord Chancellor sitting in Lincoln's Inn Hall. Implacable November weather. . . .**

[159]

Dogs, undistinguishable in mire. Horses, scarcely better;
splashed to their very blinkers. . . . Fog everywhere.

Dickens used these "crisp, tasty sentence fragments" to draw
us into the story, observed Donald Newlove in his critical collection *First Paragraphs.* He noted that the fragments in *Bleak House*
"fire us instantly," before a buildup of long, complete sentences
that suggest the novel's atmosphere of literal fog and legal obfus-
cation.

Fragments that paint a scene in small flashes, as in the Dickens
passage, are perhaps the most common type in journalism and literature—second only to those used in dialogue. These scene-
setters are like fragments in a stage direction, eliminating such
verbiage as *one sees* or *there appear* and simply presenting the subject's relevant elements: *A cheap hotel room. Disheveled writer at window. Flashing neon sign outside.* But there are scene-setters, and then
there are scene-setters. See how beautifully Sandra Cisneros, a
sentence artist, uses fragments to establish a scene in her novel
Caramelo:

Acapulco. In a house shaped like a boat. Everything curled like
the fronds of a fern. The ocean. Our hair. Our sandals drying in
the sun. The paint on the boat-shaped house.

And she knows when to stop. Lesser writers produce exhaustive lists: *A hotel room. Mini-bar. Liquor miniatures. Canned mixers.
Packaged cheese. Salted nuts. Candy bars. Corn chips. Dips.* OK, we
get it—now shut the door!

For high-pitched scenes, writers often call on fragments to
suggest breathlessness and urgency. In bodice-rippers, when passions dare not speak their verbs, the prose tends to gasp in fragments:

Her mouth. Welcoming. Eager.
His shirt torn. The steely muscles.
His longing.
Together. Now and forever.
Bliss unimagined.

I can tell you from experience that hacks love the paragraphed fragment for the way it eats up space. But writers at all levels take advantage of the fragment's energy. In *A Heartbreaking Work of Staggering Genius,* novelist Dave Eggers let it add a touch of the manic to his protagonist's musings:

> But she looked like she had a boyfriend. Did she? That secure look. So at ease. Not just a boyfriend, but a good man, too. A large man maybe. A boyfriend who lifts heavy things for a living. Or could, if he wanted to.

In *The Life of Pi,* novelist Yann Martel mixes fragments with short sentences when the hero finds his cargo ship breaking up in a storm:

> Inside the ship there were noises. Deep structural groans. I stumbled and fell. No harm done. I got up. . . . I had gone down just one level when I saw water. Lots of water. . . .

Such fragments are natural and forceful. Their task is simply to advance the drama in small parcels. But problems can arise when fragments are overburdened; when they are asked not only to add some information, but to help us keep track of who, what, where, and how. Consider, for example, the following passages from two novels I enjoyed overall, but whose fragments I found wearing:

[161]

Up in the burying ground under the starlight. Full of pie and boiled beef. A hard freeze coming down. The sky jellied with light. Little sips of whiskey. . . . Another sip of whiskey. Shaking his head. (—Jeffrey Lent, *In the Fall*)

A barely there morning. A mean-thin trickle of water from the shower nozzle. A breakfast of cornflakes no choice and white bread, no choice and Vegemite, no choice and Bushell's tea and instant coffee. . . . Dave talking loudly into the emptiness of how he wants to be a cool dad. (—Nikki Gemmel, *Alice Springs*)

The punchy writing styles of today could hardly exist without fragments, which help create the conversational style. But writing is not conversation, which benefits from such nonverbal cues as voice quality, body language, and timing. Even digital conversation has its codes, emoticons, and other means of inflection. Conversation can proceed almost indefinitely using fragments propelled by cues. Writing cannot. To hold its readers, writing needs more of the clarity that comes from named things doing named acts: Sentences.

TWENTY-ONE

THE POETRY OF LISTS

Can you identify this list of particulars from a novel that shocked America in 1958?

> [F]our books of comics, a box of candy . . . two cokes, a mani-
> cure set, a travel clock with a luminous dial, a ring with a real
> topaz, a tennis racket, roller skates with high white shoes, field
> glasses, a portable radio set, chewing gum, a transparent rain-
> coat, sunglasses . . . swooners, shorts, all kinds of summer
> frocks.

In Vladimir Nabokov's *Lolita,* these are among the items that Humbert Humbert buys to appease his preteen inamorata during their infamous road trip across the United States. In structure, this is simply a list; but like a Greek chorus, its particulars chant the pathos of Humbert's warped adoration.

Lists find their way into every type of writing: into poetry, as parades of images; into fiction, as revealing inventories; into journalism, as persuasive details. Mystery writers pan crime scenes for particulars, nature writers harvest whole landscapes, food writers empty the larder (as do many literati; see sidebar below, "Particulars on a Platter").

[163]

Form / Life Between the Marks

Young authors pump out lists with unstoppable gusto: the grungy contents of a room, a character's gross body particulars. But too often the vitality of such lists dissipates in their insistent overkill. "Yes, yes—we get it," readers find themselves thinking. But restraint is difficult. Writers fall in love with their collections of telling items. And, of course, the more items, the less meaning each has to deliver.

But lists of particulars do indeed deliver—or can, when treated more like poetic elements than laundry lists tacked to the narrative. One of the holiest mantras of creative writing is, "favor the concrete over the abstract, the particular over the general." Nothing beats the power of a concrete particular to stir associations and feelings. But many writers—their journals overflowing with painstakingly observed particulars—rush to unload them by the bushel. And so we get lists such as this one from the novel *Hourglass* by Danilo Kiš, enumerating the garbage along a jetty:

> [A] melon rind, a tomato, a half-eaten apple, bloated cigarette butts, a dead fish, crusts of bread, a dead rat, a box of matches, a squeezed half lemon, a rotted branch, a pinecone, a toothpick, a few wisps of straw, fish scales . . .

And the author goes on and on, listing some twenty-three more items. The widely admired (but to me, unreadable) Kiš has been called "a master of lists,"—and indeed, he's been known to spin them out as long as two hundred items. But only the tortured souls who inhabit his novels would counsel other writers to do the same.

A long list is usually an indulgence. As stimulating as each individual item might be, the procession can become as tiresome as a Tournament of Roses parade. The problem may be more than one of overload. Something that so disrupts the narrative pace needs a purpose—other than showcasing the author's collectibles. The particulars need to play off of one another, or build to a crescendo; they might serve to create an atmosphere or unveil layers of character, but something should give them special, collective force. Call it the art of the list—a way of composing the particulars you've so lovingly gathered.

A LOUSE CRACKED IN TWO

Reading Mario Vargas Llosa's *The Storyteller,* I came across a passage—itself featuring a list—that presents a self-contained principle for list making, a hint for sorting out which particulars are worth listing. In the novel, an itinerant teller of stories to Amazonian tribes explains what sustains him as he walks the lonely jungle trails:

> I start listening. And I learn. . . . After a while the earth feels free to speak. It's the way it is in a trance, when everything and everyone speaks freely. The things you'd least expect speak. There they are: speaking. Bones, thorns. Pebbles, lianas. Little bushes and budding leaves. The scorpion. The line of ants. . . . The beetle, as well. The little stone you can hardly see. . . . Even the louse you crack in two with your fingernails has a story to tell.

"The things you'd least expect speak." There it is: an unveiling of the force that resides in the unexpected and painstakingly observed particular. In listing, we often reach for the most symbolic items, the ones that seem to shout loudest—the dirty socks, the gold-plated Cadillac. But sometimes the less a particular speaks

[165]

in its everyday existence, the greater its voice when coaxed into dramatic context.

In his novel *The Corrections,* Jonathan Franzen compiles a list of some twenty particulars to illustrate the divide between a daughter and her mother. The items have little to say on their own as they sit gathering dust in the mother's basement. But how poignantly they speak when the hot-wired daughter, by throwing out "her mother's crap," attacks the parent's hated frugality:

> [T]he Korean barfleberries, the fifty most obviously worthless plastic flowerpots, the assortment of sand-dollar fragments, and the sheaf of silver-dollar plants whose dollars had all fallen off. . . . The wreath of spray-painted pinecones that someone had ripped apart. . . . the brandy-pumpkin "spread" that had turned a snottish gray-green. . . . the Neolithic cans of hearts of palm and baby shrimps and miniature Chinese corncobs, the turbid black liter of Romanian wine whose cork had rotted . . . the collection of Paul Masson Chablis carafes with spider parts and moth wings at the bottom, the profoundly corroded bracket for some long-lost wind chimes.

SOUNDS AND TEXTURE

Some inventories win the day by sheer quality of word and phrase. When poets list particulars, they usually treat them as, well, poetry. They choose terms with stimulating qualities in addition to their contextual relevance. Not to obsess on garbage, but from a long poem of that name by A. R. Ammons (*American Poetry Review*), I extract a few such terms that appear in various small lists throughout the work:

[B]roken-up cold clams . . . crippled-plastic chair . . . beach
goo . . . gobbet . . . eroded roads . . . flits of steel . . . shivers of
bottle . . . busted slats . . . spinningly idle wheels.

Writers can bring the same poetic qualities to enumerations in
prose. When a list by comedic writer Mark Leyner (*Et Tu, Babe*) is
set as poetry, one sees that his seemingly out-of-control particulars are well under the control of a word artist. Here, I've broken
up his prose thumbnail of a Jack LaLanne Health Spa into lines of
verse:

> *Yelping aerobics classes,*
> *the echo of raquetballs,*
> *sweaty florid-faced hausfraus in garish leotards*
> *   lumped at juice machines,*
> *men with hairy jiggling breasts and*
> *   gelatinous rolls of stretch-marked belly fat*
> *grimly tramping on treadmills and Stairmasters.*

This, by the way, is a list containing some ten particulars
(counting those found in modifying clauses), a number that feels
just about right for achieving the desired effect. Fewer items, and
the list would lose its manic thrust; more and it would seem gra-
tuitously mean.

Often you'll find that the old "rule of three" applies to lists of
particulars. To indicate a house furnished "usuriously," for example, Andrea Lee (in her *New Yorker* short story "The Birthday Present") has her doted-upon protagonist glance at a "Piedmontese
Baroque cabinet in the dining room, a watchful congregation of
Barbie's in the girls' playroom, a chubby Athena in a Mantuan
painting in the upstairs hall." Three items, and we get the picture.

[167]

PARTICULARS ON A PLATTER

As lists of particulars go, nothing seems to inspire writers and stimulate readers more than edibles. The best such inventories gather words so sensual you can chew them. In *The Middleman and Other Stories,* for example, Bharati Mukherjee offers up "platters of mutton croquettes, fish chops, onion pakoras, ghugni with puris, samosas, chutneys."

Once writers open the food locker, however, they have a hard time closing it. Sometimes a long list is justified by the significance of the event—say, a wedding feast amidst the bleakness of ranch life:

> [P]ork barbecue, a baron of beef pit-roasted, spitted lamb, prairie oysters, sweet corn, giant shrimp in Tyler's ketchup sauce, oven rolls, a keg of sour pickles, melons, ripe Oregon peaches made into deep-dish pies, and a three-tier wedding cake with pale-blue frosting topped by a tiny plastic bull and cow. (—Annie Proulx, "The Bunchgrass Edge of the World")

I'm not sure we needed the whole shopping basket, however, when Bill Bryson's hiking companion, Katz, stocked up for the Appalachian trail in *A Walk in the Woods:*

> [F]our large pepperoni sausages, five pounds of rice, assorted bags of cookies, oatmeal, raisins, M&Ms, Spam, more Snickers, sunflower seeds, graham crackers, instant mashed potatoes, several sticks of beef jerky, a couple of bricks of cheese, a canned ham, and the full range of gooey and evidently imperishable cakes and doughnuts produced under the Little Debbie label.

Well—on second burp, maybe we did need the lot. The more the funnier, it seems, when the gag is about excess. And, in massively large part, a character is what he eats.

NUTS, BOLTS, SCREWS, STAPLES

Here are some mechanics of composing lists: Note that in the short story excerpt above, Lee omits the word *and* before the last item in her series. This is the standard way to indicate that a list is not definitive—that the items are just samples pulled from a greater inventory. Use *and* if a list represents the author's essential "take," as it does in Jon Lee Anderson's snapshot of a Taliban mullah's compound in "After the Revolution," a piece that appeared in the *New Yorker:* "The bedroom, which is small and dank, has a ceiling fan, a double bed, and two white-and-faux-gilt mini-chandeliers."

For better variety and force, try to avoid the static *to be* and *to have* verbs in your lists. Instead of, *there were three lemurs, four parrots, and one python in the room,* try something like, *the room sheltered three lemurs . . . ,* or *a python eyed four parrots and a trio of lemurs across the room.*

But sometimes a list wants to be a true list—an unabashed inventory of particulars with collective impact. In Composition 101, such lists usually follow an introductory statement and a colon. The items are separated by commas, or by semicolons if complicated in structure. Some contemporary authors (or their editors), however, disdain the semis. Novelist William Kennedy's inventory of a prostitute's parlor (*Roscoe*) sets up with the colon, proceeds with commas only, and breaks—as lists often do—with a dash to introduce a summary clause. Kennedy writes of

the plush decor established by her decorators: George III armchairs, pink linen drapes on the windows, marble horse figurines on the marble coffee table, a baby-grand piano given to Mame by an ardent customer, a portrait of Mame as a young beauty—in sum the escalation of Mame's sense of herself.

In literature, the list itself might be thought of as a kind of parlor—not necessarily of ill-repute, but a showroom of particulars chosen for the occasion. Visitors ought not to be besieged by quantity, but rather engaged by the choicest items or the ones they least expect. Even for paying customers, more is not always best.

TWENTY-TWO

THE ART OF THE SEMICOLON

Even outside the world of punctuation, the year 1644 was not without its moments: Sweden declared war on Denmark; the Manchu Dynasty replaced the Ming in China; philosopher René Descartes declared, "I think, *ergo,* I am." But for lovers of semicolons—and no few roam the planet—the year leapt into history when British schoolmaster Richard Hodges offered these words in *The English Primrose,* his notable pronunciation and spelling guide: "At a comma, stop a little. . . . At a semi-colon somewhat more."

Our modern semicolon had settled into the English language.

Until then, it appears, no authority had nailed down a role for the mark in English, though its use in Latin had been somewhat standardized (see sidebar, "The Saga of the Semicolon," below). And once put to work in the English sentence, the semicolon showed Copperfield-like ambition, becoming what some now call our most sophisticated punctuation mark.

But in its very sophistication, the semicolon has caused unease among both beginning and practiced writers. "I exist, *ergo,* figure me out," it seems to say. This unease may be part of a renewed self-consciousness about punctuation, reflected in the immense popularity of Lynne Truss's 2003 best-seller *Eats, Shoots & Leaves: The Zero Tolerance Approach to Punctuation.*

As it turns out, Truss's intolerance applies more to humorless prigs than to adventurous semicolons—about which she left several trenchant things unsaid. For leaving them to be said here, and for reminding the multitudes that punctuation can be a beautiful thing, we thank her, moving on now to our own look at the art of the semicolon.

ARTFUL OPTIONS

Why do we refer to the "art" of the semicolon? Because nuance and personal style, not grammatical convention, guide many uses of this mark today. Many of the old conventions or "rules" for semicolons, perpetuated by such esteemed writers of their times as Henry James, have faded. The few standard models remaining apply mostly to specific cases, such as semicolon use with a series of *whereas* clauses. The rest is art—a matter of optional choices.

When does the semicolon option arise? Mainly when closely related statements yearn to be united, rather than exist as a sequence of jerky sentences. Consider these two statements: *She dated five men that year* and *by December she was still alone.* To join them you could use the conjunction *but,* preceded by a comma: *She dated five men that year, but by December she was still alone.* Or you could apply the art of the semicolon, creating just enough suspension for the reader to feel the poignancy of the connection: *She dated five men that year; by December she was still alone.* Each choice, in the appropriate context, yields a different feeling: usually subtle, but sometimes as different as major and minor keys.

THE SAGA OF THE SEMICOLON

Near the close of the fifteenth century, Venetian printer Aldus Manutius took a thousand-year-old punctuation mark and, in his Latin texts, standardized it more or less as the modern semicolon. Within decades, English writers were using it to pieces. Hamlet might have acted sooner without the 574 semicolons Shakespeare strewed in his path.

Weaving in and out of favored English grammar, the semicolon became the darling of nineteenth-century rhetoric. But individual writers have gone their own ways in using the mark. Dickens loved the semicolon and fussed over it. Shaw wrapped it in his own ironbound rules. In America, Mark Twain made ample use of it to pace his sentences. President Lincoln called it "a useful little chap."

Most newspaper editors feel that semicolons slow a story, but that they are tailor-made for headlines: *WRITER SELLS POEM; QUITS DAY JOB.* William Zinsser (*On Writing Well*) finds the semicolon a bit musty, as does a fictional editor in John Irving's *A Widow for One Year:* "No one knows what they are anymore.... If you're not in the habit of reading nineteenth-century novels, you think that the author has killed a fruit fly directly above a comma."

But the majority of modern writers turn to the semicolon for clause-heavy lists and for joining related statements in a lyrical, sometimes soulful way. And of course some writers use it for almost everything. Ms. Truss (among others) warns against the mark's addictive pull; but she asks: "How much notice should we take of those pompous sillies who denounce the semicolon? I say, none at all."

ASK WHAT SEMICOLONS CAN DO FOR YOU

To link statements, one has several options besides the semicolon or the conjunction. Even when the statements issue from world

Form / Life Between the Marks

leaders, punctuation can be up for grabs. During his 1961 inaugural address, President John F. Kennedy uttered these famous two clauses, pausing briefly between them: "And so, my fellow Americans, ask not what your country can do for you [*pause*] ask what you can do for your country."

But how is that pause to be represented in print? Check enough quotation books, and you'll find five different marks competing for the job: comma, dash, period, colon, and semicolon. Which best suits the message? Obviously the call is a subjective one. My own judgment would be based on these considerations:

- The comma seems too hurried, too trivializing, as if one were saying: "Ask not for the large pizza, ask for the small one."
- The dash is too abrupt. With a dash, one expects an indirection, like, "Ask not what your country can do for you— ask how you can get heartburn relief."
- A period (full stop) allows time to anticipate the locution and to think, "Yeah, yeah, I get it."
- And a colon warns of some tedious enumeration: "Ask not what your country can do for you: Ask what you can do about poverty; ask what you can do about the environment; ask what you can . . ."

The semicolon seems just right as a bridge between the two echoing clauses. It calls for a brief rhetorical pause, as before a punch line. It announces that the two clauses will relate, but it doesn't give away how. Will there be an elaboration? Question? Statement? Command? Any of these could follow a semicolon, but not necessarily. With the semicolon, there is a split-second tease. In music, certain effects raise expectations of related ones: Notes go up; we expect they'll come down. One set of beats anticipates another: *Shave-and-a-haircut; two bits.* Semicolons inject expectation into sentences, and in literature expectancy is a good thing; it creates subliminal tension followed by release: the quiet "ah" of art.

In his much quoted "Notes on Punctuation," essayist Lewis Thomas likened the glimpse of a forthcoming semicolon to "climbing a steep path through woods and seeing a wooden bench just at a bend in the road ahead, a place where you can expect to sit for a moment, catching your breath." A semicolon does indeed promise a mini-pause, a chance to gather oneself before moving forward. But it isn't always refreshing. Toni Morrison's Pulitzer Prize-winning novel *Beloved* is awash in semicolons that weigh like sighs as the author writes of slavery's horrors: "Two were lying open-eyed in sawdust; a third pumped blood down the dress of the . . . woman."

Sometimes, instead of a pause measured in time, the semicolon creates a mental space, enabling readers to take in image-loaded passages like this one by David Foster Wallace:

> I can make out in the stands stage-left, the white sun-umbrella of the Moms; her height raises the white umbrella above her neighbors; she sits in her small circle of shadow . . . a delicate fist upraised. (—*Infinite Jest*)

An excess of such spaces, of course, can get spacey. In a noted critique, semicolon-hater Paul Robinson decried the "epidemic" use of the mark by students. He objected to the ambiguity of semicolons. What precise relation do they indicate? he demanded.

[175]

But one curmudgeon's ambiguity is another's poetry. What semicolons *can* indicate are certain nuances felt by the writer, certain gestures and whispered messages. Perceived in a split second at the end of a clause or poetry line, semicolons say things like: "wait"; "brace yourself"; "take stock"; "here's more"; "here's a stronger way of putting it"; "here's how"; "here's why"; and "come along, I'm waiting for you."

DEEPER SECRETS OF SEMICOLONS: SOME QS & AS

What is "parataxis"?

It sounds like a name for unlicensed cabs, but *parataxis* is the rhetorical term for the joining of sentences, phrases, or clauses without the use of conjunctive words such as *and, but,* or *because.* And here's where the semicolon comes in: Often it substitutes for these conjunctions, giving a different feel to the locution. Which of the following two is more lyrical—or less dweeby?:

Conjunctive: Run away with me, since I need you.
Paratactic: Run away with me; I need you.

Can semicolons be used within quoted dialogue?

Yes, just as commas and dashes are used to approximate two kinds of spoken pauses. A semicolon might represent a pause somewhere between the two: "Folks come; folks go," she answered. (Toni Morrison, *Beloved*)

Semicolons are used to separate wordy items in a series. But what about a series of one- or two-word items?

Use semicolons if the intent is to convey significant spoken pauses. For example, when a lawyer listed one- and two-word afflictions that his client allegedly suffered, he used semicolons to create a "sympathy" pause after each one:

SPUNK & BITE

"[He suffered] . . . headaches; vertigo; nausea; hypertension; scalp tenderness; insomnia; mood dysphoria; photosensitivity; and phonophobia." (—John Cassidy, "The Misery Broker," *The New Yorker*)

When semicolons are used to separate items in a series, can a comma be used before the last item?

Yes. Use either a semicolon or a comma, but be consistent. Wilson Follett (*Modern American Usage*) prefers a semicolon before the last item, but later authorities cite a trend toward commas. Just be sure that clarity isn't lost: *She tried switching computers; she wrote by hand; she dictated to a recorder, her old one from work, and she prayed to her muse. Nothing helped.*

Can a semicolon be used between two sentences joined by a conjunction (and, but, etc.)?

Yes. If Wordsworth (among thousands of others) can do it, why not you?:

> *The Child is the Father of the Man;*
> *And I could wish my days to be*
> *Bound each to each by natural piety.*

This particular pattern is common in poetry: the semicolon indicates a pause between lines, where the second line launches a sentence with a conjunction. In prose the semicolon occurs after a long sentence or complicated one, offering readers a pause before a conjunction that picks up the flow: "All right, I'd yea, yea and oui, oui and si, si and see, see them too; and I'd walk around in their guts with hobnailed boots." (Ralph Ellison, *Invisible Man*)

What is the proper placement of the semicolon in relation to quotation marks and parentheses?

Outside the marks:

> *She told me, "Forget semicolons and get a life"; I didn't answer.*
> *She told me to forget semicolons and get a life (in so many words); I wish I'd said something.*

[177]

What are some special (optional) uses of the semicolon?

Here are three:

1. To set up sarcastic phrases with a loose *that* or *this*: *"To thine own self be true"; that and three bucks will get you a cup of coffee.*

2. Before introductory words like *namely* and *specifically: For you, we encourage a program of therapy; namely, get a job.*

3. Between echoing statements, especially brief ones: *A writer proposes; an editor disposes.*

VARIETIES OF CONVENTIONAL USE

As useful as they can be, semicolons are but one instrument of expression among a multitude. Some writers prefer to fashion expressive pauses and connections with other devices, limiting semicolons to a few conventional uses. Bill Bryson uses mainly commas (and correctly anticipated laughs) to break up his complex sentences. In *A Short History of Nearly Everything,* semicolons are almost entirely absent—except in such standard constructions as this:

> [H]e observed that there are three stages in scientific discovery: first, people deny that it is true; then they deny that it is important; finally they credit the wrong person.

This particular use—in a series of statements or items (usually set up by a colon)—is the one we all learned in Composition 101. It is especially handy when several of the items in the series carry their own punctuation, such as commas:

But man, could we kiss! We kissed for hours in the busted-up front seat of a borrowed Chevy, which, in motion, sounded like a broken dinette set; we kissed inventively, clutching our boyfriends from behind as we straddled motorcycles, whose vibrations turned our hips to jelly; we kissed extravagantly.
(—Diane Ackerman, *A Natural History of the Senses*)

Semicolons are used mainly for clarity in such series, separating extravagant chunks of prose (if not eager teenagers). But in literature they can also act as a sort of mortar, helping to create cumulative effects, as in this chilling passage from *Beloved:*

Whole towns wiped clean of Negroes; eighty-seven lynchings in one year in Kentucky; four colored schools burned to the ground; grown men whipped like children; children whipped like adults.

Other conventional uses include placement of semicolons before "transition" words such as *therefore, however,* and *nevertheless* when they come between statements (*The dog ate my manuscript; otherwise, I'd be famous.*); and the semicolon to set up ellipses, which denote missing verbs or other parts of speech (*Hemingway wrote standing; Capote, on a couch; Rostand, in a bathtub.*). Grammarians used to say: Don't use the semicolon unless the statements are complete (i.e., with a subject and verb) and a period could have been used instead; and use a semicolon only if the period seems too strong and the comma too weak. But few modern authors worry about how complete the statements are, or think in terms of weak and strong. Their concern is: How do I want to orchestrate the sense and cadence of my writing?

[179]

TWENTY-THREE

DARINGLY QUOTELESS DIALOGUE

I don't think of myself as a control freak. But when I read a story, I like to know (a) where dialogue starts and stops, (b) who is speaking, and (c) which words belong to the speaker and which to the narrator. Is that so uptight?

"Well here's a thought," says my inner wiseguy. "Behold the *quotation marks.*" "Well, duh!" I reply. Of course I know that quotation marks frame dialogue—as they do here, and as they've been doing in English prose for at least three centuries. Along with paragraph breaks, they are the reader's road map—the key to understanding who is speaking when.

"But tell me, Wiseguy," I persist, "if quote marks are so informative, why are fiction writers dumping them left and right?"

Wiseguy and I then continue our dialogue, but without quotes: Dumping? Who says? Look for yourself. Quote marks? Yes—and paragraph breaks, too. Not to mention dialogue tags. Why is that? You tell me. No, you tell me. I—You—Wait— Help! *Who's talking here?*

That's just what I wondered recently as I neared the end of an acclaimed new novel. I'd found the book sluggish except for its dialogue, which so far had been dutifully flanked by quotation marks. But now, when I most needed to follow the conversation, those marks went on break; the dialogue style got sneaky. Artful. Minimal:

> Those are empty words at times like this. For you perhaps, Captain, perhaps that is the difference. I only want to know facts, After that we can decide what he was. You mean *you* can decide, It should be clear I have decided already.

Yeah, whatever, I thought, losing interest. This particular patch of dialogue happened to involve a shadowy figure, so it might have seemed like a good idea to ghost out quote marks and paragraph breaks. But for me this passage, and others like it, grew as murky as the jungle river snaking through the tale.

Unmarked dialogue is nothing new, especially when the speakers are somehow disembodied. In many a twentieth-century work, characters floating through someone's thoughts prattle without quote marks or paragraph breaks. The stream-of-consciousness style, for example, has become almost de rigueur since Molly Bloom's soliloquy in James Joyce's *Ulysses* (1922): "I used to go to Father Corrigan he touched me father and what harm if he did where and I said on the canal bank like a fool."

But what about dialogue between tangible, flesh-and-blood characters? Why are so many writers reinventing the style? Browse through a heap of contemporary fiction, mainstream or small-press, and you'll soon find dialogue that flouts the standard rules of punctuation and form. Among American novelists, the flouters include Cormac McCarthy, Alice Walker, Stephen Ambrose, John Edgar Wideman, Anita Shreve, Charles Frazier, Louis Begley, and Frank McCourt.

The quoteless style got a boost in 1955, when McKinley Kantor used it throughout his Civil War novel *Andersonville:*

Form / Life Between the Marks

Judah set his wide thin jaw. I feel rested like.

I'll go down myself.

What in tunket! You just finished your chore.

Having written screenplays and a verse novel, Kantor might have felt that quote marks cramped the spoken word, much as Pablo Picasso once viewed punctuation as "the fig leaves that hide the private parts of literature." And after *Andersonville* won the 1956 Pulitzer Prize for fiction, who could say Kantor was wrong?

LITERARY EDITORS ON QUOTATION STYLE

What do literary-review editors have to say about quotation style? Editors of three far-flung reviews, each of which had published fiction with quoteless dialogue, were asked for a few words on the topic. They offered these comments:

Christina Thompson (editor, *Harvard Review;* writing instructor):

> We are definitely seeing more stories that do not use quotation marks when indicating speech. And, speaking for myself, I have no inclination to try to restore the marks, so long as it is clear who is speaking. Here at *Harvard Review,* we probably wouldn't tolerate dialogue that doesn't break to a new paragraph with the introduction of a new speaker; that seems to me a convention worth holding onto. But we're fine with pieces that don't use the inverted commas.

Ronald Spatz (editor, *Alaska Quarterly Review;* author; writing instructor):

> Although the use of dialogue that is not framed by quotation marks or dashes is not new, I have not observed any trend in that direction. The

success of such a stylistic device, of course, depends on whether or not it is organic to (and in service of) the overall work. If it works against the intent of the piece, then it's going to strike the reader as gimmicky or worse. If it works in an integral way, then it becomes a part of the fabric of effective storytelling.

John Tait (fiction editor, *American Literary Review;* author, writing instructor):

I think enough of a precedent has been set by now (Joyce, Gertrude Stein and Faulkner come to mind) that irregular dialogue formatting is not only acceptable these days, but may even feel a little hackneyed or derivative rather than edgy or avant garde.

I usually tell writing students that, if they choose to break standard conventions, they just need to be sure there are more pros than cons. The most obvious con is clarity, of course. Since most of the dialogue conventions are purely functional rather than anything else, they just need to find some alternate way of ensuring speech is clearly rendered and attributed (i.e., that there's little confusion over who said what and what is speech and what is narrative).

I have read some fiction, more in a postmodern or experimental vein, where confusion and lack of clarity are deliberate (or where I've been told they're deliberate), but I'm often a little suspicious in such cases unless I can see some immediate powerful or provocative effect that makes me forget my confusion.

LEAVING THE COMFORT ZONE

Who can say *anyone* is wrong for trying alternative styles? In writing, *wrong* means only the failure to connect with one's audience. Ordinarily, devices such as quote marks help standardize communications and avoid confusion. But if breaking with convention jolts an audience without bewildering and losing it, then perhaps something right is in the air. How should one proceed? Writers have to gamble that the hoped-for effects will neither confuse nor alienate readers—not to mention editors. A rebellious style that misses its mark simply looks affected.

Convention is there to be upended; but it is never to be taken lightly—especially in dialogue, one of the great reader-comfort zones. At the sign of the quote mark, gray slabs of narration give way to broken lines and shorter paragraphs—to refreshing pools of white space. The format signals the reader to sit back, take a break from the narrative voice, and listen to characters given life by those twin upside-down commas—or, in England, by single quotes; in France, by guillemets (<< >>); and elsewhere, by dashes and other marks.

Yet, some writers find good reasons to disturb the peace. They may discomfort audiences, but they deliver art worth the grief. Among those who do so consistently is Nobel Prize winner José Saramago. The Portuguese novelist weaves his unmarked, often unattributed dialogue—as in the small excerpt following—into passages of Olympic length and majesty:

> How are you, reversing the situation, for surely it was up to him to express interest in her state of health, I'm fine, thank you, and quickly added, I wanted to know if you're feeling better. (*The History of the Siege of Lisbon*)

Saramago works the style so ably that, after fifty pages, a more standard format would seem distracting.

Less accomplished writers might hit or miss when they buck conventional dialogue style and drop its paraphernalia. When they hit, they score effects like these:

- *intensity:* stripped-down dramatic tension;
- *tautness:* exchanges so tight the punctuation seems squeezed out;
- *speeded-up pace:* as if the speakers' pauses had been deleted;
- *dreamlike mood:* pure word flow untainted by marks and tags;
- *integration with narrative voice:* creation of a you-are-there effect;
- *imagined or contemplated speech:* absent the signifiers of "sound";
- *poetic quality:* the feel of free verse; and
- *"modern" look:* a streamlining that some editors (not most!) seem to like.

One can take small risks or large. At the small end would be, say, substituting an initial dash for pairs of quotation marks, as Charles Frazier did in *Cold Mountain.* He still employed dialogue tags and paragraph breaks to guide the reader:

—How old are you? Inman said.
—Eighteen, she said.

A riskier technique, as pioneered by McKinley Kantor, is to use tags and paragraph breaks, but no marks to signal speech. Lately this style has been so linked to Cormac McCarthy that one critic dubbed it "literary McCarthyism"—an unintentional knock on a style that investigates art and not Communists. And then there's the big risk: dropping not only quotes, but also attribution tags and paragraphing. Writers considering this approach

[185]

should be their own toughest interrogators, grilling themselves through the reader's eye, asking,

> "What's the point?" or
> —What's the point? or

What's the point? I don't know, you tell me. No, you're the author.

SPUNK & BITE

Clarity

"A HOUSE OF GREAT SPICKNESS AND SPANNESS"*

---

*Seamus Heaney, from remarks at a reading

TWENTY-FOUR

THE FENG SHUI OF WRITING

Skeptics and scoffers, lend me your ears. For when it comes to exotic fads, I'm out there scoffing with the loudest of you. Mystical cures for writing woes? Fuhgetaboutit. Ancient eastern astrology? I'm rolling on the floor. Even when my writing turns to slag, you are not likely to find me mining the *I Ching* (Book of Changes) for advice.

And so I scoffed when an artist friend suggested that I plunge into *feng shui* (pronounced "fung shway"), the ancient Chinese system of arranging one's environment for maximum flow of *ch'i,* the so-called universal life-force. But I decided to dip a toe into the subject when this good friend insisted that an "unblocked" working space might energize my writing, as it did her art. She claimed to have bettered her fortunes by placing certain feng shui devices—wind chimes, mirrors, plants, and red objects—in strategic nooks of her studio. I did more or less the same in my study.

Ideally I would have gone for the classical feng shui setup: a country dwelling aligned with the forces of nature. Its north end would have been tucked into a protective hill, with its southern frontage descending to a river (ch'i likes flowing water). But for expedience, I built a funky little fountain next to my city sidewalk.

Clarity / "A House of Great Spickness and Spanness"

Encouraged by a run of five or six good sentences, I continued dipping into home-oriented feng shui sources; and as I did so, I achieved my enlightenment (actually more of a *duh*): I realized that feng shui's principles—of harmony, balance, uncluttered paths, and unseeable natural forces—might apply directly to writing. By pointing out blockages, feng shui might suggest channels of powerful, liberated energy. Writers might track the flow of force in their sentences or stanzas and overall compositions.

YIN MEETS YANG

Feng shui (literally "wind" and "water") is a cherished principle of Asian architectural and interior design; it calls upon practitioners to consider the interaction of all things and the creative tension between their "feminine" yin and "masculine" yang qualities. Yin is said to be the cool, dark, solid force; quiescent, passive, and contracting—in contrast with the hot, bright, diffusive yang, an active and expansive energy.

The Western world treats feng shui faddishly—as a commercialized New Age trend—but also as a discipline to be studied, akin to acupuncture in its complexity. That complexity should not discourage writers—who, after all, are not about to design the next Imperial Palace. Rather, feng shui can be seen as a guiding metaphor; writers can employ its basic concepts in examining their work and in composing passages that flow with energy. Even as novices, they can identify the *shar-ch'i,* or "killing-breath" forces, that subvert positive ch'i.

I stick to the simplest principles here—because, frankly, I am not the genius to superimpose feng shui profundities on the architecture of language. We await some master to do it. Meanwhile, if in the spirit of feng shui I can help a few writers direct

[189]

more ch'i through their paragraphs, it will bring me five happinesses. Maybe seven.

A RIVER OF CH'I FLOWS THROUGH IT—OR TRIES

Once they are viewed as furnishings, the elements of any sentence invite appraisal using feng shui (henceforth *fs*) principles. From books on my shelves I've plucked a few sentences whose elements suggest good and bad *fs*. Though not perfect examples, the selections might serve as points of departure for exploring the ch'i of expression. Each sentence is taken from a superior work by a stellar writer; and while the ch'i flows freely in some sentences, in others it feels blocked:

> After stopping for a maximum cholesterol breakfast—buttered hotcakes and sunny-side ups—at a place called Hobo Joe's, in the blink-and-you-miss-it town of Madill, I travelled ten more miles, until I came upon a gymnasium-size building, with a cream-colored metal exterior, set back about a hundred yards from the highway. (—Mark Singer, "The Chicken Warriors," *The New Yorker*)

Think of that sentence as a little house. Among other things, good *fs* demands:

- an easy entrance into a clutter-free first room;
- good vibes (or "cured" vibes) from past inhabitants or previously owned furnishings;
- yin and yang elements in harmony;
- ch'i-attracting objects or patterns placed where they are most purposeful;

- ch'i-draining objects (like flushing toilets) situated where they will do the least harm; and
- a winding, smooth-cornered path (known as a channel or meridian) through which ch'i can flow freely and leisurely.

Now what about the sample sentence quoted above? Dependent clauses do not necessarily make for bad "entrances," but the clutter of this opener gives me trouble; I must stumble through a distracting aside, hyphenated adjectives, and five loud images before reaching the low-energy subject and its verb ("I travelled"). The phrase "maximum cholesterol breakfast" feels previously owned, trailing negative energy as if from some health newsletter.

The pathway to the sentence's exit is also clogged: more hyphenated adjectives; a pileup of images; and descriptions of distance, dimension, and direction, all jerking the mind's eye this way and that.

The sentence does what writers are always urged to do: It uses concrete, sensory images, which are generally more stimulating than abstractions. But images are powerful ch'i-attracting "objects"; *fs* can help guide their placement. For me, the power of "buttered hotcakes" overwhelms the blink-and-you-miss-it imagery that follows. Is that bad *fs,* or was I just hungry?

Fs is hardly an exact science. Codified, yes, but varied within its several warring schools. Western practitioners tend toward flexible, subjective approaches. Below are two other food-minded sentences that, in my subjective view, seem more hospitable to ch'i:

That fried bread's aroma, a lilting thread of nearly crystalline or caramelized air rising to the upper floors (smoke curling in cat's-cradle configurations up the stairs and under the doors of

[191]

the rooms where her sisters were sleeping), roused the ever-plump and food-loving Irene from her slumbers, and this sister, in a great flannel gown and with red ribbons in her pigtails, soon had made her way into the kitchen. (—Oscar Hijuelos, *The Fourteen Sisters of Emilio Montez O'Brien*)

Here the strong image ("aroma") is the subject, welcoming ch'i into the first "room" of this compound sentence. Parentheses slow it momentarily, but lush modifiers and sibilant sounds carry the ch'i through sensual curves and curls until the yang-ish verb ("roused") ushers it toward the yin-ish object ("Irene"). When the sentence veers into its second room ("and this sister . . ."), it does so at a natural, gentle angle. The ch'i is drawn onward by the color red—the magnetic, fire-element color—and it exits through the kitchen.

According to the *fs* principle of "like attracts like," each positive element in the sentence seems to attract others, just as one disruptive element would do damage beyond itself. Offensive elements, such as outdated and sexist terms, can generate so much shar-ch'i for a reader that they function as ch'i drains—much like that flushing toilet.

Here's the other culinary sentence:

It's something to see, the way she concentrates, her hot, busy face, the way she thrills to see the dish take form as she pours the stewed fruit into the fancy mold, pressing the thickly cut bread down over the oozing juices, feeling it soften and absorb bit by bit a raspberry redness. (—Carol Shields, *The Stone Diaries*)

[192]

Okay—if we present any more soft-bread imagery we'll soak up all the ch'i. But again, the sensual object of the sentence is well placed, receiving action within a smooth flow of activity. The opening clause is like an invitation, a door thrown open to ch'i. Simple but concrete language carries the force along until it hits "oozing juices." This potent phrase comes close to creating a ch'i "pool," a junction so energized it bottles up the flow. But to the rescue comes "raspberry redness," once again employing the draw of red, that magnetic color. The sentence's parallel structure and mirror-like repetitions also beam the ch'i forward, deflecting it from potential sticking points.

FENG SHUI "CURES" FOR BAD-CH'I WRITING

Through intricate means, feng shui attempts to cure the disrupted ch'i of one's living space. Its tools include colors, scents, and live plants; powerful or heavy objects; mirrors; and sounds, such as chimes.

Such tools have many analogues in writing, among them color, scent, and nature imagery; forceful verbs and weighty nouns; "mirrored" (echoed) words, sounds, and constructions; and euphonious words and sound combinations.

Often one "power" word in a sentence releases the ch'i of an entire passage. I remember coming across such a word in a news story on border-town traffic. Just as the piece was getting bogged down with details, the sentence "Diesel fumes marinate the air" uncorked its ch'i. The hot yang verb "marinate" was perfectly placed in the context of the whole.

Many are the *fs* cures and their variations. But when syntax hits the wall, when emphasis is muddled and meanings blocked, the best fix may be to re-furnish the house; that is, bring in new elements and rearrange everything. The following sentence (from a newspaper editorial) might need such a cure, with its impossible angles and ch'i-draining components: "By struggling to find ways to overcome patterns that exclude the differences that make life worth living, he developed a vision that is consistently unethical."

[193]

Clarity / "A House of Great Spickness and Spanness"

Bear in mind that a sentence, though handy as a model for applying feng shui, is but one small element of flowing prose, one rivulet in the landscape. It is the whole work that must sit in the "belly of the dragon"—the feng shui metaphor for a perfect house setting.

THE FENG SHUI CHECKUP

Intuition traditionally plays a part in applying *fs* to landscapes and dwellings. But fitting environmental principles to prose and poetry is essentially an analytic process, an editorial act. In this respect, writers should check their work for sound *fs* principles well apart from the act of creation. To block creative flow with any left-brain editorial process is bad *fs.*

Once in the analytic mode, poets can examine such ch'i-sensitive elements of their verses as piled-up images and line breaks, while prose writers might attack these ch'i-unfriendly elements, among others:

- excessive parenthetical asides;
- a monotony of "straight-line," or simple, sentences;
- clichés, dead metaphors, and worn-out phrases;
- dangling participles and misplaced modifiers;
- subject-verb disagreement;
- shifts in tense;
- relentless use of passive voice.

As I name these grammatical terms, I can hear the scoffers asking, "Well, isn't *fs* just a lot of mumbo jumbo when it comes to writing—or does it really tell us something that, say, *The Elements of Style* doesn't?"

My answer is that only a personal exploration of *fs* will tell. For me, *fs* has added a concrete, palpable dimension to the principles of clarity presented in *The Elements of Style*. It has helped me balance Strunk and White's yin approach with a more aggressive yang point of view. But there remain a zillion aspects of *fs* that are beyond my ambition to extrapolate, and which we leave untouched here: Among them are the critical interrelatedness of fire, earth, metal, water, and wood (and their symbolic equivalents), and the importance of the *bagua*—a type of diagram that maps the flow of energy within nine life areas (including wealth, fame, luck, and health).

So who can say what new insights *fs* brings to word arrangement? For skeptics, the more answerable question might be: Do guides like *The Elements of Style* reveal anything that feng shui practitioners didn't understand some three thousand years ago?

TWENTY-FIVE

HUNTING DOWN DANGLERS

Glancing through The New York Times *obituaries the other day, the face of a recently deceased thespian caught my attention.*

As this sentence of mine alleges, a dead actor's face did indeed catch my attention the other day. But according to how the sentence actually reads, that face did a creepy something else: It rose up from the newspaper to cast theatrical glances at the surrounding obits.

How is this the case? Because, although the sentence starts off with a clause about what *I* was doing ("glancing through the obituaries"), the word *I* never shows up to perform the action. Instead, *face* appears as the subject, so that logically only *face* could do the glancing. Devious, isn't it?

Had "I," the true glancer, made an appearance, the actor's face could have rested in peace. But, alas, I allowed a modifying phrase ("Glancing through *The New York Times* obituaries the other day") to dangle—to sit there all by itself, without the target ("I") it was intended to modify. As a result, I let down the phrase, the sentence, its readers, everyone. That's what danglers do.

To make amends, I would offer rewrites such as, *Glancing through the* NYT *obituaries the other day, I spotted the face of a recently deceased thespian,* or, *Appearing in the* NYT *obituaries the other day, the face of a deceased thespian caught my attention.*

We pride ourselves on making beautiful matches between our subjects, verbs, and modifiers. Yet dangling verbal phrases and other forms of misplaced modifiers are popping up in all the best-edited media, not to mention in such usual haunts as student writing, conversation, and sportscasting. Simply seek and you will find them, perhaps even in a piece you're readying for submission. Danglers may not mark the end of civilization, but they sully our little corner of it.

YEARNING MODIFIERS

Back, back, into grammar class for just a second. Remember participles, those modifying words derived from verbs? In the sentence *Writing madly, she didn't notice the killer,* for example, *writing* is a present participle that modifies *she;* and in the phrase *A book written for money,* the word *written* is a past participle, modifying *book.*

Often a participle finds itself controlling a group of words, which is then called a participial phrase. For example, the participle *writing* controls the participial phrase *Writing her quota every morning,* which appears in the sentence *Writing her quota every morning, she soon had three chapters.* Can you see how the whole participial phrase, controlled by a verb form, yearns to modify something in a nearby clause—something to perform the action? No wonder the nearest noun or pronoun is often grabbed for the job. But in our sentence, because the controlling participle is *writing,* it has to modify a subject that actually *does* the writing. When that logical subject is missing or misplaced, the participle dangles. Consider this sentence: *Writing her book every morning before the kids arose, the strain was more than she could bear.* Can a *strain* write? I don't think so. The phrase is a dangler.

And so the hunt for dangling participles is on, at least for us early rising writers. Some observers hunt them mainly to fatten their list of howlers—"Slathered with cream cheese, she brought the bagels to her handsome neighbor"—greeting them with a "haw, haw." But I encounter them ruefully.

Why ruefully? Because it vexes me to see participial phrases, one of our language's most elegant constructions, so corrupted. Participial phrases may be overworked in journalism, where some writers, for the sake of varied structure, haul them into every few sentences: *Appearing before the judge, she. . . . ; Dressed in a three-button suit, he . . . ;* and so on. But at their best, they function like stage sets, yielding a dramatic rush for the reader as the curtains part and a sentence begins. Their flash of background or setting illuminates the forward action. With a pleasing rhythm, a participial phrase swings into the heart of the sentence—or extends it meaningfully, like a coda:

> "And I was daily his delight, rejoicing always before him."
>
> (Proverbs 8:30)

They contribute to the music of a beautiful complex sentence:

> Passing the yellow-spear'd wheat, every grain from its shroud
>   in the dark-brown fields uprisen,
> Passing the apple-tree blows of white and pink in the orchards,
> Carrying a corpse to where it shall rest in the grave,
> Night and day journeys a coffin.
>
> (—Walt Whitman, "When Lilacs
> Last in the Dooryard Bloom'd")

SPUNK & BITE

There, in Whitman's lines—see how the participial phrases modifying "coffin" keen the movement of Lincoln's funeral procession across the states? Had those phrases dangled, the corpus might never have reached its place of rest.

Find-the-Dangler can get a bit tiresome when focused on ludicrous results, as it so often is (*Opening the casket, Lincoln seemed almost alive*—get it?) But in literature, correct participles transfer emphatic power or grace from modifier to target. Missed targets are missed opportunities, not just logical fumbles. On we go, then, deeper into misplaced-modifier territory to spot the thieves of emphasis—but also to identify the danglers we can leave alone.

COURTING TROUBLE

Glancing through the nation's newspaper of record the other day, then, I found not only the usual depressing news, but also the dolorous presence of a dangler. And once I began paying attention, I found several more danglers over the next few months, both here and in other shrines of American prose style. Often the slips were subtle and certainly understandable in deadline journalism—but they underscored the perils of modifiers once-removed from their logical targets. Such modifiers include not just participles, but also forms like this one, found on an editorial page:

> With jurisdiction over a range of family issues, including adoption, divorce, domestic violence, child custody, and juvenile delinquency, Family Court's caseload has swelled enormously.

Did you notice who has all that jurisdiction? The writer meant to communicate that Family Court does; but the subject actually being modified is "caseload." This, Captain, is illogical; the "with" phrase is a modifier hooked to nothing that makes sense. It dangles.

Two common problems sabotage the logic of the sentence. First, prolonged modifying leads to forgetfulness by the time the main clause comes along. Second, a possessive ("Family Court's") upstages the subject. A similar example: *After talking to the philodendron every day for a week, including evenings, when she would add a prayer, Aunt Amelia's plant began to perk up.* (But not to talk to itself or a fellow philodendron, as the sentence, whose subject is *plant* and not *Aunt Amelia,* states.)

Danglers are tricky devils within a demon class known variously as "hanging," "unattached," "wandering" "misplaced," or "misrelated" modifiers. Like creatures who assume human form, they take on familiar shapes in our sentences, sometimes even animating them and conveying thoughts. More mischievous than malignant, they still have no business corrupting good sentence design.

WHEN GOOD MODIFIERS GO WRONG

Here's the surest way to see if a modifier is wonky as used in its sentence. Identify the subject being modified, and stick the modifier right *after* it. Then ask, "Would the sentence make sense if written this way?" For example, take this sentence heard on National Public Radio: "Unlike other national holidays, most Americans go to work on Martin Luther King Day." Now the test: "Americans, unlike other national holidays, go to work on Martin Luther King Day." The result is one big "huh?" in need of a rewrite. Try your rephrasing skills on these examples, too:

- "As a valued Preferred Customer, your order has been double-checked for quality." (—President, Seattle Filmworks, promotional literature)

SPUNK & BITE

- "Other than impending baldness, the future looks bright for Moby." (—*Illinois Entertainer*)

- "Inserting the uprights, the rudimentary plan of an outsize four-poster began to emerge." (—Redmond O'Hanlon, *Into the Heart of Borneo*)

- "By lifting the hips, the trousers were pulled free." (—John McGahern, *By the Lake*)

MEN WHOSE MODIFIERS WANDER

The sentence sounds perfectly idiomatic: *To understand men, one thing has to be remembered.* But as so often happens in sentences opening with an "infinitive phrase," there is no subject to carry out the action of the infinitive verb. In our example, *"thing,"* is the only subject, here incapable of understanding men or any other topic. Little wonder that men are poor misunderstood creatures, or that danglers sneak into their manuscripts, applications, and corporate advertisements. (Well, into women's, too.)

A recent full-page ad promoting *The Wall Street Journal,* for example, featured an executive crowing about meticulous copywriting. One would expect perfection here, in an ad pertaining to writing skills. But instead, the executive dropped a dangler to this effect: "After working as writer and creative director, Pat F invited me to visit F_____ M_____." What he'd meant was, "After *I* {not Pat F_____} had worked as a writer . . ." The executive probably got to keep his job anyway; but for lesser job seekers, a single dangler in a cover letter may be one too many. I once received a cover letter from an applicant claiming twenty years of communications experience. It included these two fatal sentences:

Clarity / "A House of Great Spickness and Spanness"

As a marketing strategist, my livelihood depended upon the time/cost value of meeting client expectations . . . I wish to use my considerable communication skills to help your house maintain high standards in grammar, spelling and sentence structure as a proofreader and/or copy editor.

The first dangler is like those so common in obituaries: *A native of Chicago, his ashes will be scattered over Wrigley Field.* (The modifying phrase searches in vain for the deceased.)

The applicant's second sentence offered to make my publishing house a better proofreader. Here is an instance of a wandering rather than dangling modifier. Why didn't the writer place the phrase "as a proofreader and/or copyeditor" next to "skills," instead of letting it wander off where it seemed to refer to "house"? Perhaps, knowing how fast applications are read, he feared slowing down the sentence before he got to the idea of helping us. But he didn't help his cause.

OH, YOU KNOW WHAT I MEAN

What's the big deal as long as everyone knows what a sentence means? Not only can danglers and other faulty modifiers convey unambiguous meanings, but often they also seem most natural to the ear. Imagine a lawyer summing up his case before a jury: "Worried about her mother's operation while driving to the hospital, the accident was something we can all understand." In spite of its dangler, this sentence clearly posits the cause of the accident. The language seems so sincere that I'm going to vote "not guilty," hoping that no one was injured. Yet, without a worrier present (i.e., a subject to do the worrying), there can be but one verdict in Grammar Court: guilty as charged.

[202]

I may be an imperfect writer when I create danglers, but what happens when I use them in conversation? Am I in deep trouble with the language mavens? Am I a cross-eyed dunce if I say, "When crossing lanes, my eyes are always on traffic"?

Hardly. Most grammarians preach tolerance of spoken danglers, which rarely create confusion about their meanings. Some authorities lament the very persecution of danglers. They argue that such constructions can be the most natural or literary way of expressing some things, and that "corrections" are often klunky. They point to differences in nuance between such statements as *lying in my bed, everything seemed so still* and *as I was lying in my bed, everything seemed so still.*

As usual, the "rules" have been robustly violated by the masters, including Shakespeare ("sleeping in mine Orchard, a Serpent stung me"). But in fact no rule against dangling verbals existed until the late nineteenth century, when rhetoricians began to hunt for such phrases and cite outrageous examples. Among modern authorities the topic has provoked spirited discussion (more than four thousand words in Follett/Barzun's *Modern American Usage* alone). All agree on a basic rule: that modifying phrases should be tethered to their intended posts; but most experts temper this rule with standard exceptions and cases calling for special judgment.

BARRING EXCEPTIONS . . .

Among the main exceptions are participles used in an impersonal sense, such as *concerning, assuming, barring,* and *failing.* Such verbals needn't link to a specific subject when they seem to modify something more—that is, when they seem to modify an entire clause: *Barring rain, the sacrifice will be held as scheduled.* Such participles often appear with the subject *there* or *it: Assuming you've read this far, there is no need to define* participle; *Concerning the future,*

[203]

it remains to be seen. These uses have become so idiomatic, say grammarians, that the verbals function more as prepositions and are excused from their verbal obligations.

Other participles in this class include *speaking, considering, supposing, looking, granting, recognizing,* and *regarding.* Even in the case of terms from this ever-growing list, however, the most meticulous writers will apply further tests to justify using them without explicit subjects: For example, they will ask, "is the participle used without *any* suggestion of an agent performing the action?"

But even these tests are imperfect, the grammarians confess, determined to leave us dangling. My advice: Unless you're a copy editor, concentrate on the clear connections between modifiers and targets—and do the concentrating during revision, not while composing. Get the jacket on first; but then, if you care about impressions, match up the buttons.

TWENTY-SIX

MAGIC IN THE NAMES OF THINGS

Every summer, to the chagrin of friends who sail, I decline invitations to come aboard and join in their revelry. Call me a word lubber, but I'm happier on dry land with my nose in a glossary of nautical terms. That way I can enjoy the salty names of all those boating objects, without having to clean or stow a single thing.

Take me to any port of nomenclature—to listed names of tools, fungi, hats, or hairdos. Such specialized lists might be the closest a writer comes to undiscovered English. Drop your own anchor in some exotic category, and there they are: warehouses of terms barely known to the general reader; a treasury of words, many of them irresistible in their sound, inventiveness, or precision.

Over there, for example, in that chest labeled "Weather and Natural Phenomena," lie semiprecious terms like *katabatic wind* (the night wind down a mountain valley) and *alpenglow* (the light that bathes a peak at sunset). Poets will walk on clouds as they rummage around.

Where exactly are these wares to be discovered? Mainly in a class of reference sources absent from the shelves of most writers. These remarkable works list the world's things and their parts by categories and subcategories. They present the nomenclature of things, usually with brief definitions; or they key the names of objects to labeled pictures. The labels, in turn, name related things or parts—say, the *gorget, pauldron,* and *cuish* of a suit of armor.

As a writer you will revel in these stores of fresh, metaphor-ready terms heretofore hogged by specialists; but such lists offer more than just pretty words. For here is where you will find the true name of that whatzit you've been trying to think of—the thingamajig you want to identify for your readers. When you must speak the language of unfamiliar worlds, these sources will serve as your phrase books.

NAMING THE STUFF OF DREAMS

Often, as I listen to the droning account of someone's protracted, inchoate dream, I wish that the speaker's dreamscape had included labels. At least then I might enjoy some of the freshness, specificity, and lyricism that comes from authentic nomenclature.

Below, a typical dream-teller struggles to describe the bizarre what-chamacallits he encountered among his A-waves. If only he had used one of the sources cited in this chapter. But with or without these types of aids, see if you can replace the italicized descriptions below with precise and sometimes lovely terms. (The numbers in parentheses correspond to my own suggestions for terms, which are listed after the passage.)

> "So I'm like floating through this city, and on top of a temple dome I see this (1) *cap-like thing with windows* and a weird dude standing inside it. Down below, this (2) *architectural whatchmahoozie above the pillars* says "Abandon All Hope." I go in anyway and I see a guy with one of those (3) *knotted-up-across-the-belly* shirts and a big tattoo, you know, like a (4) *cross with three-leaf clovers on the ends.* He calls me in

this (5) *deep, all-esses-and-tees, high-class* voice. He's holding something over his eyes, sort of like a (6) *pair of glasses on a handle sans side pieces.* The dude has one of those (7) *big bulby noses* and a (8) *tiny patch of beard right under his lip.* And I'm like pouring sweat from that (9) *little dent between my nose and mouth.* Suddenly the dude (10) *makes a whole bunch of quick running steps* toward a light coming from this (11) *humongous round hole in the dome.* He turns to me and lowers the glasses–thing, and there's his eyes sliding open, except they're behind these (12) *inside eyelids like cats have!* Wow, I like scream so hard that—you know the little (13) *hunk of flesh that dangles over your throat?* Well, that little sucker is shaking like a (14) *thing inside a bell.*

My suggestions: 1) lantern; 2) architrave; 3) calypso; 4) botonée; 5) plummy or plumy; 6) lorgnette; 7) cob-noses; 8) barbiche; 9) philtrum; 10) scuttles; 11) oculus; 12) nictitating membranes; 13) uvula; 14) clapper.

KNOWING THE THINGS OF WHICH YOU WRITE

You cannot always write what you know, but it helps to know what you write. You might set out to write a sailing scene without knowing what to call the thingamabob that swings loose and knocks folks across the whatchamacallit; but in the act of writing, you'll need such terms.

In her novel *The Shipping News,* E. Annie Proulx had to refer to many parts of a boat, including the *trim, transom, tilt latch,* and *self-bailing drains.* Had she not known these terms, she could have found them in the various nomenclature-reference tools that cough them up as needed, even as they fatten a writer's general stash of descriptive and metaphorical terms (not to mention crossword puzzle answers).

Name-listing sources include universal and specialized glossaries, picture dictionaries, and occasional lists within thesauruses and reverse ("flip") dictionaries. The Web? Yes, one can also ride the search engines to online glossaries, while facing the usual challenge of extracting the well-edited and reliable from the thousands of worthless hits. Combine *sailing* and *glossary* in a search and you'll eventually find such collectible terms as *alee, burgee, luff, monkeyfist, vang, yawl,* and *scupper.* You'll also find *spanker,* whose assonance-rich definition is "a gaff-headed sail attached to the mizzenmast." (*www.pacificoffshorerigging.com*)

Specialized glossaries, however, tend to be most comprehensive and useable in their full-blown print versions. For the thousands of volumes that won't fit on my shelves, I rely on libraries. But one multi-themed glossary will never be out of my reach: Stephen Glazier's *Random House Webster's Word Menu,* the paragon of omnibus name lists.

Glazier's story epitomizes the labor of love behind great word collections—a passion for language that is palpable to anyone who luxuriates in its results. A novelist and magazine writer, Glazier died at age forty-four, shortly before his three-thousand-page manuscript of *Word Menu* went to press in 1992. He spent some twenty years of his life gathering the names of things and hammering out brief but authoritative definitions for each. He developed a special system of classification to help modern writers and others find the things they knew or thought existed but couldn't name. Although Glazier's masterpiece sometimes seems to be a well-kept secret among language lovers, the determined seeker can find *Word Menu* (revised) in libraries and bookstores. The digital software version is also available online at *www.wordmenu.com.*

Glazier's typical menu within a category is extensive, if not exhaustive, and shows his writer's eye for choice terms. His "Ships and Boats" menu, for example, includes such pearls as *bumboat, dink, felucca, gufa, vaporetto, xebec, rat line, cat's paw, swabby, wigwag, buttock,* and *futtock.* A typical concise definition looks like this:

> **thole** pin set vertically in gunwale as fulcrum for oar.

Aye, a trace of blood on the thole—thar's been mischief at sea, I'd wager.

Under the volcano: More name sources

With that, we will move on from things nautical, except to mention that nautical terms appear in other types of whaddyacallit sources, including these two worthy compilations:

- *Descriptionary: A Thematic Dictionary,* by Marc McCutcheon; and
- *The Describer's Dictionary: A Treasury of Terms and Literary Quotations,* by David Grambs

Like Glazier's guide, these two sources differ from most thesauruses in that they list whole inventories—and not just synonyms—under a category, in addition to defining each term. In the "volcanoes" entry, for example, *Descriptionary* provides no synonyms for *volcano* itself. Instead, it offers the names and definitions of volcanic things—*obsidian* (volcanic glass) and *lahar* (hot ash flow), among other mellifluous-sounding items. The book's index makes it easy to check a half-known term, as well as find a dozen more good ones. I followed *crankshaft* from the index to the "Automobiles" inventory, where I learned that *creeper* is the thing mechanics lie on to roll under a car.

Lexicographer Grambs's *Describer's Dictionary* approaches the names of things by means of the qualities that define them—a reverse dictionary of sorts. For example:

Clarity / "A House of Great Spickness and Spanness"

Rocky debris on a mountain slope: scree.

Qualities are grouped within broad "common sense" categories, and sometimes it takes a little browsing to find the desired one. Browsing, however, is the delight of this work, for opposite each page of qualities and terms are choice literary passages using the same or similar terms: "They crossed a stone stile on to the moor . . . with the screes of the mountain rising steeply on the left." (Bruce Chatwin, *On the Black Hill*) Of particular use to writers are sections listing physical and personality features of people. Here you can find the term for that bulbous nose, for example, that you want to pin on a character.

THINGS LITERARY

When it comes to nomenclature of the world's things, some names seem neutral or klunky while others have qualities that writers find irresistible. Such qualities include newness to the general reader (*tombolo,* for example, referring to a sand bar connecting an island and its mainland), appealing sound (*sassafras*), and concision (*dew*). But perhaps the most intriguing quality of certain names is aptness—an exact, right-seeming match between word and thing.

In *I'm a Stranger Here Myself,* Bill Bryson has some fun with words that seem perfectly suited to the items they represent and those that seem all wrong. While *granola* sounds like it should refer to crunchy bits of cereal grain, he says, the word *muesli* conjures up a salve for cold sores, or even the cold sore itself. Among other perfect words—words so perfect that no one has to tell you what they mean—he cites *globule, snooze,* and *dribble.*

What makes a word seem apt? Linguists theorize that humans create words for certain things by mimicking the things with their lips and other speech organs. The moon, for example, is mimicked by the shape of the lips as they form the "oo" sound of *moon*—or *luna* or *lune.* Naturally the words seem apt.

Other words, like *buzz* or *clang,* aptly imitate the sound or feel of the things (see Chapter 11 for more on *onomatopoeia*). But how many words can be produced by mimicking? Perhaps the more a word reflects the dynamics of early language formation—whatever that might have been—the more apt it seems to us. Yet so many older words disappear, displaced by neologisms that seem equally apt.

While linguists ponder such mysteries, writers can rely on instinct as they pore over the names of specialized things. They will know which apt ones to pounce on for literary use: exotic words like *djellaba* (North African hooded robe), used by novelist Nicholas Christopher in *Franklin Flyer;* or sturdy ones like *testudo* (a protective shell formed of shields in Roman battle), employed as a metaphor for a firm back in Seamus Heaney's poem "A Shiver."

And because names bestow poetry on the ordinary, writers will raid even commonplace categories for such words as *jalousie* (slatted shade or door), *petiole* (stem of a leaf), and *tang* (knife end to which a handle is attached).

Compiling *That Book: . . . of Perfectly Useless Information,* Mitchell Symons raided glossaries for a few "Names of Things You Didn't Know Had Names." Okay, some of them are arguably useless to writers—like the name for the armhole in a shirt or sweater (*armsate*). But when Symons offers names that sound just like what they are—*rowel,* which refers to the revolving star on a spur, or *nittles,* the punctuation marks denoting swear words in comics—my lips form little *oos* of satisfaction. And there's nothing useless about that.

PLEASE READ THE LABELS

Often a labeled picture is the shortest distance between the blank in a writer's sentence and the name of a thing. If the thing can be represented graphically and is not specialized beyond the mid-geek level, there's a good chance it appears in one of linguist Jean-Claude Corbeil's visual dictionaries (for example, the *Macmillan Visual Dictionary*).

Corbeil's editorial teams label tens of thousands of pictured objects and components with their most common names. Are you describing a crisis in a coal mine? You'll find an illustration in one of Corbeil's dictionaries, crisp and diagrammatic, showing the exact location of the *stope, adit,* and *winze*—places where miners could be trapped.

Or perhaps you're writing a backstage thriller. Your villain has positioned himself high on the thingamajisser from which heavy stage objects can be dropped. Turn to the appropriate line drawing in another visual reference—a book from the Oxford-Duden pictorial series—and there's the term you're looking for: *fly floor,* or *fly gallery.* Moreover, this Dutch series includes bilingual editions, so if your hero declaims in French, he can shout *"la passerrelle de service!"* as per the *Oxford-Duden Pictorial French & English Dictionary.*

These or similar "pictionaries" are easy to find in library or bookstore language sections. Got a birthday coming up? Ask for a deluxe edition like Corbeil's *The Firefly Visual Dictionary,* or *The Ultimate Visual Dictionary* by Jo Evans, with color plates that will blast your sclera through your superciliary arch.

TWENTY-SEVEN

THE EARNESTLY ENGAGING SENTENCE

Like the protagonist of a moral tale, a sentence sets out in earnest pursuit of truth and beauty. But soon it finds itself set upon by corruptive elements, which must be vanquished before the glorious end punctuation is attained. Yea, many a foul flaw have I seen befall a virtuous sentence; and many pieces of writing (my own darlings among them) have I seen the worse for it.

Yet it all seems so simple: A subject. A mighty verb. Perhaps an object that receives the action it deserves. A well-placed modifier for a bit of the old nuance. A pretty clause or two fluttering like silk ribbons. But step back to admire your creation, and—*aargh!*—the slithery thing is devouring its tail.

Into every author's life come bad sentences. By themselves they may not sabotage a masterly work—but they can surely get in the way of writing one. Unstable sentences can set off chain reactions, especially for unstable young writers. The sentence goes awry, the paragraph stalls, the work deflates; the writer is last seen playing marimbas at a subway stop.

Not that every sentence has to promenade down a fashion runway; forced beauty creates its own monstrosities. A sentence has this job to do: Move the work one step forward without tiring, confusing, or sidetracking readers. If it needs to evoke feelings, it

[213]

Clarity / *"A House of Great Spickness and Spanness"*

does so without a choir of mewling clauses. In tandem with other sentences it builds drama and creates rhythms and harmonies; it contributes to the flow and engagement of a passage and ultimately the work.

Here, for example, are a few compelling sentences from two books full of them:

> And so she tuned out the tour guide and heeded the October angle of the yellow light, the heart-mangling intensity of the season. In the wind pushing waves across the bay she could smell night's approach. (—Jonathan Franzen, *The Corrections*)

> Once, he'd seen, through the bedroom window, a tree come shockingly into bloom. Its leaves had been bluish gray, and on that day it had given birth to an explosion of small yellow puffy balls as big as marbles, thousands upon thousands of them all at once, so that almost instantly a lemon-colored haze had filled the room. (—Anita Shreve, *The Last Time They Met*)

SORTING OUT THE PEANUTS

Bad things happen when we unload our jam-packed thoughts like a box of Styrofoam peanuts. The box is emptied, and *ah,* that feels good for a moment. But the contents are all over the place. Controlled sentences—take a deep breath here—*deliver precise language in an emphatic arrangement based on logic, economy and clarity, all to engage the reader.* (Exhale.)

These are the qualities we seek in a polished sentence. How do we achieve them? We can begin by tuning in to our instincts as readers. We would not be writing if, as readers, we had not been stirred by good sentences and irritated by poor ones. We know the difference. We believe, as language critic Wilson Follett did,

[214]

that "no one should ever be called on to read a sentence twice because of the way it is constructed."

When it comes to sentence repair, we can lean on certain structural frameworks associated with g-g-*grammar*—but let's not tense up at the G-word. We needn't understand retained objective complements to fix most problems. Just by putting a skilled reader's ear to our drafts, we'll be able to tell whether a sentence

- strikes like a cobra, or strangles its parts boa-like;
- swings open and clicks closed, or feels unhinged;
- has parts that interlock, or that fly off in different directions;
- is dramatic in its simplicity, or monotonously devoid of texture; or if it
- soars on the wings of imagery, or collapses under its own mass.

Read your key sentences aloud. Does your intent, your emphasis, come across? If not, what detracts from it? A weak verb? A clause too many? Related elements placed too far apart? Notice the sound quality of your words, and whether they fit your intent. Fine-tune the rhythms to your ear's delight, using soft pauses (commas), harder pauses (dashes, semicolons, colons), and variety in sentence length and complexity.

Pay attention long enough, and you'll be the Mozart of sentence structure, impishly celebrating one triumph after another.

A SENTENCE MAKER'S MANTRA

I have a mantra for writers who let poor sentences pile up like bad credit accounts. As you sit down to write, try this chant: "When bad things happen to my sentences, I will take control."

Trouble begins when unstructured word clusters get dumped from brain to page. It would be nice if they assembled themselves into tight sentences, or even into stream-of-consciousness prose. But these brainloads are like ideas churning in a cement mixer; out they come to glop up our sentences. They distort what we intend to emphasize, even if some meaning manages to trickle through.

Yes, we need to get sentences—any sentences—into a first draft. The trick is not to fall in love with their problems, not to consider them natural and inviolable expressions of the soul.

Are we calling for a Strunk-and-White-style crackdown on inspired outbursts? No. We say go with the outbursts, but control the problems that cause them to implode. Some writers attempt the prose equivalents of Jackson Pollock paintings—brain droppings from a ladder, so to speak. The few who succeed compose their sentence splatters in ways that direct attention and sustain interest—even the interest of editors.

YOU BE THE EDITOR: GOOD WRITERS, FLAWED SENTENCES

Here, from six good books by distinguished authors, I've culled six sentences I consider faulty, even when read in context. Can you tell how each one distorts the author's intended emphasis, or forfeits the reader's engagement? Some of these sentences should have been rewritten as two or more, some made into confetti.

- "She killed a man, he was only thirty-two." (—Janet Fitch, *White Oleander*)

- "That in the belief that a woman had to be beautiful, and sensuous, and witty, and wonderful, in order to trigger real love, erotic love, the kind of emotional drama that ran through to the heart of the universe, the hot line to the source of love itself, the in-love kind, Alexandra had been wrong." (—Fay Weldon, *Worst Fears*)

- "What his private hopes for her had been she did not know and so could not read if he was reconciled or relieved but either way she knew he was engaged now in an action called for not so much by the fact of her as by some theory of conduct, a notion of comportment." (—Jeffrey Lent, *In the Fall*)

- "I spent a frantic couple of hours pacing in my room—that is, I'd come to think of it as 'mine' but it wasn't really, I had to be out in three weeks, already it seemed to be assuming a heartless air of impersonality—and drafting a memo to the financial aid office." (—Donna Tartt, *The Secret History*)

- "Days to come they rode through the mountains and they crossed at a barren windgap and sat the horses among the rocks and looked out over the country to the south where the last shadows were running over the land before the wind and the sun to the west lay blood red among the shelving clouds and the distant cordilleras ranged down the terminals of the sky to fade from pale to pale of blue and then to nothing at all." (—Cormac McCarthy, *All the Pretty Horses*)

- "The issue of the relevance of the truth-value of the beliefs that a poem expresses faces in two directions: towards the poet and towards the reader." (—Malcolm Budd, *Values of Art*)

COMMON FLAWS AND FIXES

What follows are a dozen sentences that need some help. For each, I've suggested fixes that would normally apply. When would they not apply? When the sentence—warts, wildness, and all—nonetheless achieves some compelling aesthetic effect. Dextrous writers like David Foster Wallace, for example, can get away with section-opening sentences like this:

> The sudden strength with which the desire to go see whether the initials I'd carved so long ago in the wood of the stall in the men's room of the Art Building were still there, the sudden and unexpected and overwhelming strength with which these feelings had washed over me, there at the dormitory, with Lenore, was a frightening thing. (—*The Broom of the System*)

Often the sheer power of image, of idea, can trump grammatical or structural conventions. Such power, however, can also work within the conventions—which themselves serve emphasis and reader-engagement.

But now for the promised clunkers. They illustrate twelve common problems in flawed writing, with suggested fixes for each:

BROKEN HINGE: She asked everyone for the meaning of life, who could answer?

FIX: A comma is a soft pause, not a stop or a gate between statements. Insert hinge words like *and, but,* or *yet,* or use a semicolon instead: *She asked everyone for the meaning of life, but who could answer?* or *She asked everyone for the meaning of life; who could answer?*

DELAYED ACTION: Ibrahim could not, in spite of all his training, knowing that the platoon depended on him, even with the armed and hated enemy in his crosshairs, fire.

FIX: Delayed (or "periodic") sentences—in which the verb and subject are placed far apart—can be suspenseful, but too often they shoot themselves in the foot. Keep the verb near its subject: *Ibrahim could not fire, in spite of all his training . . .*

DULL VERBS: There were loud cries by the customers for more Krispy Kremes.

FIX: When the advantage is clear, get rid of dull *there-are* constructions and let subjects act through live verbs: *The customers bellowed for more Krispy Kremes.*

ACTIONLESS ACTION: She had a yellow forked tongue. Its papillae were poisonous.

FIX: *To have* and *to be* are actionless verbs; use stronger ones: *Her tongue unraveled, yellow and forked. Poison oozed from its papillae.*

OVERCROWDING: He mowed the lawn, ran into the house, answered the phone, listened as his wife yelled and the dog scratched on the door, made a chicken sandwich, stopped thinking about what his son had said to him yesterday, and opened a beer.

FIX: If all that action seems hard to absorb, break up the sentence into smaller ones. Some teachers cite an odd "rule of three," which says that no more than three actions should occupy the same sentence. But often a long string of actions projects a feeling—a buildup of stress, an escalating madness. Had the last phrase above been *and shot himself,* all that buildup would have made sense,

[219]

and we'd have had a fine emphatic sentence—if a weepy one.

MODIFIER OUT ON A LIMB: Having climbed that tree so long ago, her memories flooded in as she touched the bark.

FIX: Make sure all verb forms refer to the intended subject: *Having climbed that tree so long ago, she touched the bark and let the memories flood in.* (For more on this problem, see Chapter 25.)

SUBJECT/VERB DISAGREEMENT: One out of every four women of that village—or maybe five—get married.

FIX: Be sure the verb finds its intended subject-mate and agrees with it in number: *One out of every four women of that village—or maybe five—gets married.*

DEADLY PASSIVE VOICE: The body was discovered in the library; later an identification was done.

FIX: Punch up interest by revealing who performed the action, making the actor (rather than what was acted upon) the subject: *A homeless woman discovered the body in the library; later the victim's fiancee identified it.*

PUNCH LINE GIVEAWAY: The reference librarian, of all people, murdered the victim.

FIX: Sometimes a passive construction (where the receiver of the action is the subject) can generate more drama than an active one by holding revelations until the end of the sentence: *The victim was murdered by, of all people, the reference librarian.*

NEGATIVE STRUCTURE: Because the publisher did not act decisively, the book was not in any position to succeed in the chains.

FIX: Rewrite dull sentences built around *not* or other negatives to allow for strong verbs in the positive voice: *Because the publisher waffled, the book crash-landed in the chains.*

WORD INFESTATION: She was of the inclination that devotion to love in and of itself was all one could ever favor, without any sort of compromise.

FIX: Eliminate emphasis-eating verbiage: *She favored uncompromising devotion to love.*

SUBJECT BLOAT: The thought that he had gained ninety pounds and was no longer the athlete that had attracted her, that she'd had to cut his toenails because he could no longer reach them, that he had lost interest in everything but feeding his face, if one could still call it a face, somehow cheered him.

FIX: A sentence's emphasis can turn on a key verb. Don't make readers slog through an endless subject to reach it: *It somehow cheered him, the thought that . . .*

Of course, the walls of every Composition 201 classroom echo with these types of reminders; and if those walls could write, they'd be something, wouldn't they? But for us itinerant word merchants, hauling sentences along the paths of corruption, every turn seems to present a new challenge. All we can do is plod ahead, chanting our mantra—and perhaps these words of Ralph Waldo Emerson:

> The maker of a sentence launches out into the infinite and builds a road into Chaos and old Night, and is followed by those who hear him with something of wild, creative delight. (—*Journals,* 1834)

SPUNK & BITE

Contemporaneity

A LEG UP ON THE COMPETITION

TWENTY-EIGHT

WRITING FOR NEW GENERATIONS

Writers—get with it! Are you reaching all those generations out there? The Boomers? The Xers? The Gen-Yers or Echo Boomers or Screenagers, or whatever they're called? And don't forget— Generation Z has arrived, albeit mostly in diapers. The wee Zers may not catch all your nuances; but soon they'll be the generation *du jour,* and you can't afford to be, gasp, Generation Yesterday!

See how the X-Y-Zs torment us? How the writer's world grows crazier? Is it history or hype that launches a new generation every five minutes? Must today's writer bust a gut playing to Pepsi's so-called Generation Next, speaking its language, dancing to its beat?

When publishers seek writers who "speak to" or "speak for" a generation, they usually mean the generation now shelling out dollars to discover itself—not your father's generation, and possibly not your own. In many publishing warrens at this writing, editors from the 50-million-strong Generation X (now in their late twenties to mid-forties) are chasing the 80 million Generation Yers (preteens to those in their mid-twenties), including some 41 million mall rats spending $180 billion a year.

Desperate to capture a share of this demographic's attention, editors look for steroidal syntax, street voice, prose with a 'tude. Television producers seek "high-octane," high-adrenaline reality programming, consigning scriptwriters over thirty to Jurassic pastures. According to *Salon,* newspapers are wording down to young audiences, believing they "do nothing but go to movies every night." And juvenile publishers, reaching for young Yers and upcoming Zers, have embraced such kid-pleasing phenomena as *manga,* Japanese comic book novels. Seeing this and other shifts to graphic literature, writers are suffering from nightmares in the shape of thought balloons.

Meanwhile, conventional writing wisdom urges us to stay calm, write within ourselves, and not chase fashions. It says to watch out for generational labels, however hot. It warns against generational stereotypes. And it counsels that assuming the communications style of a younger generation, except in dialogue, is likely to ring false.

Yet, who can ignore audience? Who can snub 80 million potential readers, their frames of reference, values, passions and sensibilities?

Even Cynthia Ozick, who feels that computers stunt writing skills and that e-mail tends toward "grunts," loosened up her style for the online *Slate:* "I was writing for *Slate,* and you write for your audience," she told *The New York Times.* Not that Ozick was writing hip-hop; but like all writers, like all editors, she had to consider the changing face of the modern reader and how (or whether) to relate to it.

GENERATIONS: A POCKET GUIDE

NAME: Boomers

DEFINITIONS AND COUNT: Born 1946–64; approximately 72–78 million

OTHER NAMES: Baby Boomers, Flower Children, Love Generation, Woodstock Generation

GREW UP: In the post-WWII age of innocence; later, in the era of counterculture, Vietnam, Dr. Benjamin Spock, suburbs, network TV, rock music, Star Trek, the Beatles, feminism, and the sexual revolution.

STEREOTYPED AS: Socially conscious, idealistic, politically apathetic, suspicious, self-analyzing, complaining.

SOUND BITE: "Dig the spirit of the struggle. Don't get hung up on the sacrifice trip. Revolution is not about suicide, it is about life. With your fingers probe the holiness of your body and see that it was meant to live." (—Abbie Hoffman, *Steal this Book,* 1971)

NAME: Generation X

Definitions and count: Generation following the Boomers. Born 1961–81; 44–50 million.

OTHER NAMES: Gen Xers, Slackers, Me Generation, Baby Busters, Yuppies, 13th Generation (of the U.S.).

GREW UP: On MTV, grunge music, punk rock, skateboarding culture, computers, Watergate, economic boom, and relative peace (except for the Gulf War).

STEREOTYPED AS: Hedonistic, socially and politically disengaged, overeducated and unemployed, job-changing, media-savvy, culturally exhausted, cynical, entrepreneurial, flip, and irreverent.

SOUND BITES: Did someone say "struggle," or were they choking on their sushi? (*Bada-boom!*) Yeah, cool, whatever. Hey, sacrifice rocks ... Not! Revolution? I'm still living with my parents. Fetch the remote, dude, we're missing *Seinfeld* reruns.

NAME: Generation Y

DEFINITION AND COUNT: Born late 1970s to mid-1990s (children of some Boomers); roughly 80 million, with about 30 million teens; racially diverse

OTHER NAMES: Gen Yers, Echo Boomers, Millennium Generation, Ritalin Generation, Screenagers, Internet Generation

GREW UP: On coddling parental care and computers; and later, on the Internet, *Ren & Stimpy, Beavis & Butthead,* video games, O. J., Monica, Valley talk, rap music, and hip-hop.

STEREOTYPED AS: Warp-speed fast on the uptake, digitally fixated, optimistic, spoiled and arrogant, impatient, multitasking, high-maintenance, materialistic, fickle, sarcastic, high on humor and irony.

SOUND BITE: Struggle? Ay yo, what's up with that, brah? IMHO, that is like totally Gen X. I'm like, "I am so not going 2 kill myself for any revolution 'less I get stuff?" Yeah, I'm down with holiness, but right now I be probing my iPod, Xbox, and cell: And you see *how* many fingers free?

And now appearing in your neighborhood . . .

TENTATIVE NAME: Generation Z

DEFINITION: Tomorrow's readers, born 2004–2025

GENERATIONS, REAL AND INVENTED

Strictly speaking, a generation is all the individuals born (and living) at about the same time. How much do people differ from one

[227]

fifteen-to-thirty-year era to the next? How much can an age group be typed?

No one denies that such broad historical events as wars, revolutions, and depressions stamp the character of generations, or that developments like the Internet shape lifestyles and attitudes. But when it comes to a generation's traits, all labeling is selective. Focusing as they do on certain conspicuous members of a population, labels ignore eternal differences between rich and poor, urban and rural, liberal and conservative, educated and undereducated, mainstream and marginal. Was everyone in the Lost Generation lost? Was every Beatnik on the road? Was every Xer a slacker? Was *any* Xer a slacker?

If generation-naming was ever culturally regulated, it has now been "deregulated," as sociologist Arlie Russell Hochschild puts it. Marketers and the media now slice off new generations as thinly as they please. Generations are identified by their digital devices, cable channels, leisure addictions; they are confused with so-called "communities," or affinity groups of mixed ages—the Heavy-Metal Community, the NASCAR Community, and so on.

And who decrees which traits will represent a generation? While Gen X and Gen Y are true population groups (see the "Generations: A Pocket Guide" sidebar, above), their defining characteristics seem to be anyone's call. If Gen Xers were slackers, why were they working eighty-hour weeks in silicon valleys? Why are so many materialistic and sarcastic Gen Yers flocking to religion?

Increasingly, generations are defying labels, inventing their own traits and even their own cycles. Authors Alexandra Robbins and Abby Wilner, have written of twenty-somethings, for example, experiencing "quarter-life crises"—burnout resulting from jobs, relationships, and the search for purpose—that mid-lifers once claimed as their own.

FINDING A HANDLE

Are writers left with anything that can at least tilt them toward a generation's affinities, help weave its codes into their syntax? Perhaps. Substantial numbers of people within a given age group do fit and/or buy into its stereotypes; they will follow certain observable patterns, as of expression, dress, and entertainment. Writers can study these patterns before attempting to infiltrate a generation's media or create representative characters.

For example, the media- and techno-savvy Yers who read *Spin* magazine expect a certain style of evaluative prose: a fusion of elegant and funky dictions, academic smarts, encyclopedic music knowledge, and street cred. Consider these snippets from various issues:

> . . . a heady harmonic-minor groove. . . . an ominous Autechre-ish pulse [that] morphs into a tightly packed metal riff . . . a history of consciousness over digitally triggered tablas and congas. . . . Imagine a Miami bass cassette in a boom box with dying batteries, with coked-up gangstas toasting beat-downs atop the noise. . . . [D]espite their hope-obliterating ennui, [they] can come strong with the stomp-box thunder . . . and sometimes you wish they'd just stick to anthemic howling. . . . recontextualized, the self-esteem is off the chain.

In the meantime, Boomer grandparents and older Xers with kids continue in their own recognizable idioms, some writers—as in these clips from *Redbook* and *Ladies Home Journal,* respectively—lingering in the still-successful mix of psychology, sentiment, and self-orientation:

[229]

Most of us females *start out* emotionally connected to other people's feelings. Our central emotional task is to develop a strong, *separate* self.

I'm loving it. . . . [My kids] need me, and tracking down footwear and translating homework is what being a mom is all about. And even now . . . after leaving the land of the solo-traveler chick and starting a family, I like the way that feels.

BEING GEN Y

Conventional wisdom notwithstanding, many a writer may want to jump the generational gap, mimicking the sound of a younger group or a special segment of it—let's say a Boomer aiming for Gen-Y-teen verisimilitude. Well, mimicking *is* what writers do much of the time; that and projecting themselves into the heads of characters and readers. Those with an attentive ear should be able to pull off at least the short bursts needed for writing effective dialogue. Daily exposure to live teens might be research enough; but for style clues, one can also study 'zines, cable shows, blogs, and other forms of teen-oriented media.

What would be learned? As it exists today, the casual speech of Gen-Y teens and young twenty-somethings—especially urban twenty-somethings—demonstrates the following salient characteristics, among many others:

- sarcastic tone; manic leaps from the serious to the banal;
- cute, patched-in catch phrases *(Hello? Can we talk about ME now?)*;
- ubiquitous intensifiers and word-compounding *(That is so totally droolworthy)*;
- black slang, Hispanic inflections; edgy raunch;

- flip and gay-influenced locutions *(Oh, look—it's Mr. Get-to-the-Pointy-Pants)*; and
- rude, impatient interjections *(And you are telling me this, WHY?)*.

Of course, casual speech is not the whole of a literary style. Young writers go well beyond hyperventilation to manifest that wired, quick-witted, stand-up-comedic quality that seems to have captivated all today's generations. Among its elements are over-the-top images, pop-culture references, jokey punch lines, subcultural vocabularies, neologisms, and twisted grammar.

Many of these traits are imitable—even by brooding Dostoevskian writers, if determined enough. To achieve more than superficial mimicry, however—to rise above stereotypes—one might have to plunge into the generational world as energetically as Tom Wolfe did for his 2004 college-life novel, *I Am Charlotte Simmons.* Wolfe, at about age seventy, toured one campus after another, infiltrating parties and observing social nuances until he felt he could get it right. Though critics caught several off-notes, Wolfe got it right enough to hit the bestseller lists, including those on college campuses.

A work like Wolfe's, set more or less in a fixed time period, is one thing; the speech patterns and likely interests of its characters can be researched and locked in place. That's how it was at the time, period. But it's another thing to capture a style that will be up-to-the-minute when read. Consider the life span of any style—a matter of days in the youth culture. Prose that attempts to be with-it today had better see print by tomorrow, or perhaps within two or three months at the most.

With books, the year-or-more turnaround time between the manuscript and print stages can curdle the voguish into the cringey, at least among trend-conscious readerships. Erica

[231]

Kennedy's hip-hop-chick novel *Bling* came out just when that term (for showy jewelry) was showing up on "enough-already!" lists. Happily, the book itself was in tune with its audience— strong in stylistic touches that, while transitory, were likely to have a few years' momentum.

BEYOND GENERATIONAL BOUNDARIES

Reaching for today's book-buying audience, writers have good reason to embrace the more engaging elements of Gen-Y style— if they fit with one's topic and treatment. Older writers may consider their usual devices engaging enough; but they still might want to filter out geezer terms that creep unintentionally into their work: terms like *dungarees, gym shoes, record player,* and others that will similarly distance them from Gen-Y readers. They might heed one of those lists that circulates from time to time, enumerating references that mean little to those born after, say, 1983: *Mork, J. R., typewriter, pry-off bottle cap, stove-cooked popcorn,* "Where's the Beef?" and so on.

To go against one's grain—to seemingly pander to another generation—will strike many writers as abhorrent. Is it really necessary for commercial success? Of course not. But relevance to an audience certainly is—and unless your language, style, or message transcends generational barriers, some fine-tuning might be in order. And some very fine tuning at that, since any age group comprises a wide variety of backgrounds, personalities, and tastes (roughly a third of Gen Y, for example, describes itself as non-Caucasian).

On the other hand, certain predilections and aversions of your age group will inevitably overlap with those of younger groups. You might well share stands on, say, the environment, war, poverty, or love. Within these commonalities, you'll cross the gap. Ilene Cooper, whose acclaimed fiction for young adults includes *The Kids from Kennedy Middle School* series, reminds us: "The emotions and worries of teens are not that much different from what they were in my day: romance, sex, bullies, parents. The difference is the lingo. But that's easy enough if you're willing to watch MTV and subscribe to *Teen People.*"

Then, too, the last thing any generation wants is a steady diet of its own voice. Though Gen-Y novelists are now blossoming, only one (Lauren Weisberger) appeared on a recent list of campus best-sellers. The other twenty-nine authors ranged from pre-Boomers (Tom Wolfe, Philip Roth) to such diverse Xers as Dave Eggers and Sophie Kinsella.

Writers have to see what works. They can stick to what feels comfortable, or they can tweak language and style to engage new readerships. But never should they abandon the fundamentals of storytelling or of poetry—those principles that have worked since Homer and *Beowulf.* Nor should writers shortchange their own passions. Yes, do think outside your generational box to connect with contemporary audiences. But tell a story brilliantly, touch the inner self, and readers will embrace your passions as well as your values—all the more so if you have relieved the soul's weariness of generational themes.

The next generation off the assembly line may be "not-your-father's-car" or your own old beater, according to those who label it. But under the hood, the forces that engage the human spirit will look pretty much the same.

TWENTY-NINE

HOT POP AND EPHEMERAGY

Determined to be every bit as punchy and engaging as the competition, many writers pepper their works with references to popular culture—the newly popular, the lingering, and the nostalgic. A seductive practice, it is also a risky one—as fizzle-prone as low-carb Pepsi or a John McEnroe talk show. (See the risk?) But when a pop reference is on the money, precise and incandescently clever, applause rolls in like royalties to P. Diddy and 50 Cent combined.

In the literary world, risk-takers can earn such admiring words as these from *The New York Times,* praising one of Mark Leyner's madcap novels: "Love seems lukewarm compared to Leyner's red-hot riffing on the ephemera of popular culture." That "red-hot" label could be slapped on to most of Leyner's work, and on to that of several other manically tuned-in authors—at least when their works first flame through this kwazy, pop-obsessed atmosphere we occupy.

But what exactly comprises the realm of "pop"? Apparently, just about everything that flashes by the window of mass notoriety: celebrities, commercial products, films and television programs, political figures, comic book characters, fashion, catchphrases, jargon, social trends, and other such transitory phe-

[234]

nomena. Building on the attractions and aversions they evoke, writers use these elements in figures of speech—metaphor, hyperbole, allusion, etc.—or simply haul them into their works for (usually comic) effect. I offer the term *ephemeragy* for all such uses of pop references. And ephemeragy, I would say, is one of the most stimulating devices in the writer's toolbox.

GET 'EM WHILE THEY'RE HOT

Stimulating indeed are the latest ingots from the entertainment mills, the news furnaces, the forges of commerce. They already spark and glow in the minds of thousands, perhaps millions, of digitally connected readers. Why shouldn't one seize upon them? Writers have always been drawn to the fleetingly popular—that's why our classics abound in footnotes. Take a figure like Bonturo Danti of Lucca, notorious in Dante Alighieri's time as a symbol of corruption, then forgotten. When he shows up in *The Inferno,* jammed into boiling pitch, Dante describes him sarcastically as the only Luccan politician innocent of graft. That, for contemporary readers, was the equivalent of saying, "He was cleaner than Enron."

Ephemeragy not only pleases an audience, but can make a writer (or a character) appear au courant, hip, with-it—the go-to source for what's hot and how to spin it. This is no minor laurel, especially in journalism. But then again, there's those risks to be considered: No matter how clear it seems to the author, a pop reference can soar over most readers' heads, or arrive so dated that the fossil who delivered it can only be pitied.

And so writers take their chances, gauging as best they can the longevity of the material and its window of exposure. Some items are fit for no more than a *Tonight* show monologue; some resonate for years, and a few become iconic. Here, for example, are some ephemeragies that tickled me when they were fresh. Take it on faith that the context set them up brilliantly; but as for staying power—well, you be the judge:

> Ryan and Travis, as the bobbing heads [of the film *Open Water*] project the manic indignation of Paris Hilton and Nicole Ritchie forced to pump gas.
>
> (—Mike D'Angelo, *Esquire*)

> "All *you're* wearing [to a Halloween party] is a black polyester suit and giant googly-eyed glasses."
> He . . . smirked. "I'm Alan Greenspan."
> I thought he was the lady from the Old Navy commercials.
>
> (—Leslie Stella, *the Easy Hour*)

> I accidentally swallowed Mike Tyson's false teeth. I can't believe it! They were gold, but money isn't the issue. . . . The problem was that Mike was planning to have those teeth set into a medallion of commitment to me.
>
> (—David Sedaris, *Barrel Fever*)

> Before this [flap over discussions of sexual preference in children's programming] is over, we're going to find out that SpongeBob is the illicit spawn of the Tampa shock jock Bubba the Love Sponge.
>
> (—Maureen Dowd, *The New York Times*)

> "You tell us what you want—which films you want Arnold Schwarzenegger inserted into and we do it right here for you. . . . you can even fax your order in and we'll deliver the Schwarzeneggerized videos to your home. . . ."

"OK. I'd like *My Fair Lady* with Arnold Schwarzenegger as Professor Henry Higgins, *Amadeus* with Arnold Schwarzenegger as Salieri instead of Murray F. Abraham."

(—Mark Leyner, *Et Tu, Babe*)

[The film *Dirty Dancing: Havana Nights* seems] like an episode of *American Dreams* written by Pepé Le Pew . . . with lines that sound as if they were spoken by Dirk Diggler in the pornomovies-within-the-movie in *Boogie Nights*.

(—Elvis Mitchell, *The New York Times*)

Why did these ephemeragies tickle me back then? How could they not, taking risible characters from pop culture and wielding them as tools of ridicule and farce? But of course, there will be no tickling of readers who are unfamiliar with Pepé LePew (the Warner Bros. Skunk of Love), or cartoon character SpongeBob SquarePants of Nickelodeon, and so on. Theoretically an author could stop to explain an item, as Dowd does briefly with Bubba the Love Sponge. But economy is crucial in ephemeragy; if you have to explain it, then you've chosen the wrong reference, or you've chosen it for the wrong audience.

To the authors of most of our examples, the pop references would have seemed relatively enduring at the time they were chosen. But things lose their notoriety or acquire a new type of it. Audiences change their points of view. A television series folds, and with it die such allusions as, "They're single again, with Felicity-esque daughters," as a *Time* staffer wrote in 1999, referencing the soon-to-be-concluded drama series *Felicity*. Each year, writers need to weed out ephemeragies based on yesteryear's headlines—especially those done to death and back again: Janet Jackson's "wardrobe malfunction," Howard Dean's "I have a

[237]

scream" speech, Martha Stewart's jail time. Or, if discarding such references is simply too painful, writers can archive them for use in accordance with the following schedule (an update of James Laver's "cycle of fashion," first presented in *Tastes and Fashion* in 1945):

The Cycle of Pop:

Today: Hot

One month old: Tired

One year old: Cringey

Five years old: Carbon-dated

Ten years old: Nostalgic

Twenty years old: Retro

Thirty years old: Classic

Fifty years old: Innocent

One hundred years old: Ur-

THE TIME RISK

Ephemeragy for the purpose of mockery—perhaps the most familiar type—runs a special risk. What if the item referenced undergoes some dark fate, such as grave illness or death, before or

[238]

soon after the mockery sees publication? The very ephemerality of pop references bids one to ignore posterity; but posterity doesn't go away. For instance, journalist Mike Barnicle wrote in 1997 that John F. Kennedy Jr. had "the body of Joe Piscopo and the brain of Sonny Bono"—forgettable, tasteless, and tragic ephemeragy, as recalled two years later by columnist Frank Rich. Barnicle's reference was mean-spirited enough in itself; but in early 1998, after a skiing accident in which the well-liked Sonny Bono died of head injuries, it seemed more tasteless than ever.

Writers can do little about the fate of their pop references, aside from wishing that the good stay good (and healthy) and the flawed stay flawed (and healthy), thus allowing the human race to continue and the ephemeragies to retain their original sense.

Of course, one can make some judgments when choosing references, treating gingerly those likely to die, break (e.g., steroidal athletes), transform themselves, or drop below the radar in the near future. As for the last criterion, the Web provides one clue to enduring mass appeal in its lists of top searches by millions of surfers. In 2005 one could learn (from the Lycos search engine) that each of the following pop "items" had been on the top-fifty list for at least five consecutive years: Britney Spears, Pamela Anderson, *Dragonball* (the anime series), WWE (World Wrestling Entertainment), and Harry Potter. Such longevity can support a choice—or its rejection in favor of fresher items: those just making the list or just starting to excite you and your particular target audience.

Writers with an eye for the culturally excessive and absurd can do without ready-made compilations of pop phenomena. But some of these lists are of interest—first, for what they reveal about the ephemeragy of a given period; and second, as a way of studying people's changing tastes. *Esquire*'s "Dubious Achievement Awards 2004" feature, for example, aims for laughs with refer-

[239]

ences to Abu-Gharib prison abuses, sexual-assault charges against basketball star Kobe Bryant, allegations of child abuse made against Michael Jackson, and the torture of Guantánamo Bay prisoners using deafening blasts of Eminem and Limp Bizkit music.

One might ask, "Must I indulge in this kind of exploitation to be punchy, engaging, and with it?" Not necessarily; trotting out the ghastly stuff is only one form of ephemeragy. In fact, among the funniest of the *Esquire* Awards was one of its most benign items; it references a horse (Smarty Jones) who was credited in the *Philadelphia Daily News* as the writer of several movie reviews. But in truth, the edgiest ephemeragy often flirts with the dark side of notoriety, either adding to that darkness or helping to purge it, depending on context and treatment.

DUMBING DOWN OR NUMBING DOWN?

Recently, comparing two dramatic performances, a top reviewer likened one to The Sharper Image, the other to Sephora. Have we dumbed down to this level in the art of metaphor—references to mall stores? But not so fast: It happened that the performances under review were television crime shows, in no loftier a cultural plane, really, than icons of the mall. And what's with all this cultural hierarchy, anyway? If a figure of speech makes a connection, it makes it. Mark Leyner would certainly agree; as he remarked in an interview with Larry McCaffery (Gopher/*Mondo 2000*),

> I despise the contemptuous attitude so many professors seem to have . . . about television, rock and roll, and certain kinds of movies. Personally I could never see the difference between Popeye and Thackeray. . . . [M]y work presents the world the way people . . . live in it, the way we receive and perceive it.

[240]

SPUNK & BITE

Perhaps the issue is not so much one of dumbing down as of numbing down. When too many pop references serve as facile substitutes for hard-wrought and more precise imagery, it begins to feel like the writer is on autopilot. In her otherwise-dead-on novel *Worst Fears,* Fay Weldon writes that "Vilna looked like a cross between a vulture and Ivana Trump," banking on what to her readers is probably a vaguely intelligible and unevocative reference. What does Vilna really look like? Come on, give us those distinctive brushstrokes that lift a character off the page and into our memories.

Poet Lisa Verigin has observed a similar effect when poets too quickly seize on pop-culture references. In "Do Elvis and Poetry Mix? Benefits and Pitfalls of Pop-Culture Poetics" (*The Writer* magazine), she grants that a specific pop or commercial reference might be more evocative than a generalized one—Adams clove gum versus chewing gum, for example. But she asks: Is such a reference germane? Does it enhance the surrounding content? Is the chosen reference essential, or is it interchangeable with others? Pop—especially nostalgic pop—can lead to sentimentality, she notes, too often manifesting itself in glops of predictable detail. Facile pop undercuts "the tension needed to drive a poem forward." To delight, surprise, and enlighten, Verigin advises, limit pop allusions to those providing something more to the poem than cause for an affirming grunt.

In prose, however, one hates to burden a pop reference with too many rhetorical and symbolic imperatives. So don't. Just deliver it with the clarity, economy, and grace expected of all good writing. Let the item and the reader's associations do the rest. A one-word ephemerage in novelist Richard Russo's *Empire Falls* tells readers exactly what the author wanted to say: "Miles studied his father, whose stubble had a strange orange tint. 'Your beard's full of food. Cheetos?' "

THIRTY

EDGE: WRITING AT THE NERVY LIMITS

The *Salon* reviewer was going on about playwright Hans Ong—"youngest recipient of the MacArthur 'genius' grant"—and his latest work of fiction. "This novel," she said, "confirms that his fierce, edgy prose translates beautifully to the written page."

Think you could you handle this praise? And I don't mean the parts about youth, genius, or MacArthur money; who cares about that junk? I'm talking about "edgy," the charged-up billing of the day, electric enough to put your name in lights—and prone to short circuits. Witness this slam of one journalist by another: "He's the archetype of the phoned-in, self-satisfied, clichéd attempt at cliché-debunking that passes for edgy prose among our calcified activist class."

Still, from the tabloid roosts to the aeries of literary publishing, editors are flapping for edgy matter—or "edge," as it is called. They want it in prose, they want it in poetry. Publicists and critics spritz the term around like chili sauce. Writers hearing the call or noting the impact of Quentin Tarantino films, HBO comedy, or the baddest gangsta rap have to wonder if they, too, should jump on the edge-wagon.

Well not all at once, please! Most editors don't expect or even want *every* writer to be edgy. But they need *some* edge to stay in the game, and a powerful dose of it can get their attention—even blast open a door closed to most newcomers. So you might well ask: Is my own work edgy? Does it need more edge? Should I focus my strengths elsewhere? And what the [*edgy expletive*] is edge, anyway?

DEFINING *EDGY*

Only recently have dictionaries recognized *edgy* as an adjective in the arts, a term meaning "bold, provocative, or unconventional." As used by today's editors, however, the word suggests something other than cutting-edge innovation or avant-gardism, which have more to do with intellectual than emotional thresholds. The literary sense of *edgy,* on the other hand, carries the full behavioral load: nervousness, anxiety, irritability, acute sensitivity. Edgy literature manifests and evokes these emotional states, but in aesthetically stimulating ways.

How does it do so? By pushing some element—situation, event, imagery, language—to the limit, toward the precarious divide between unease and displeasure. Unease makes for intensity in art; the more the better—until it crosses the line into turnoff territory.

Here, walking that line, is one of today's edgier novelists describing a patient-holding area in a London hospital. Not for the squeamish:

> [In the] long, lowering, warped spine of a tunnel . . . connecting all the various organs of the hospital . . . [one feels] . . . weighed down by the . . . effluvia of the disease itself. A rambunctious river of pus and gleet and ichor; a cascade of mucus and bile and gall. An impressively engineered Victorian snotqueduct.   (—Will Self, *How the Dead Live*)

Maybe edge is what Aristotle meant by "catharsis," tragedy's purgation of pity and fear—which I never quite grasped. To characterize edge, I would use the terms *nervously stimulating* or *irresistibly nervous-making*.

Many of today's fine writers—among them Sandra Cisneros, Zadie Smith, and Z. Z. Packer—take their stories to nervous places without trying to make the telling itself edgy. Although their vocabularies in matters of race and sex do register on the edge-o-meter, readers gasp mainly at story and character—for example, at a fed-up teacher about to run down a bunch of kids at a crossing in Packer's "Our Lady of Peace."

Often it's a writer's mix of language, style, and other elements that achieves edge. A devious plot can push the nervous limits; so can dicey protagonists, breakneck pacing, radical points of view, and flirtation with legal and personal risk. Bad-mouth a few sacred figures or crime bosses and you'll have edge—and maybe a horse's head on your pillow the next morning.

But let's talk about the two elements of most concern to the wordmeister: language and the style of its delivery.

EDGE: A BRIEF HISTORY

Edge has been around as long as storytelling; but edgy material has gone by different labels, among them *possessed, fevered,* and *outrageous.* In every literary era, someone has pushed language to its jittery edge. For fourteenth-century readers accustomed to Latin, the use of Tuscan dialect in Dante's *Inferno* had to have felt edgy. Shakespeare wrote lines that made hemoglobin nervous: "Will all great Neptune's ocean wash this blood / Clean from my hand? No, this my hand will rather / The multitudinous seas incarnadine." (*Macbeth*)

The mid-twentieth century saw the edgy darkness of science-fiction and fantasy writers, and the turmoil of the Beats and existentialists: Jack Kerouac's breathless *On the Road* prose—"and me swearing at myself for all the time and the money I'd wasted, and telling myself, I wanted to go west and here I've been all day and into the night going up and down, north and south"—and the gnawing understatement of Albert Camus' *L'Etranger:* "Maman died today. Or yesterday maybe, I don't know." Readers encountered the defiant edge of J. D. Salinger's troubled teen in *Catcher in the Rye:* "[T]he first thing you'll probably want to know is where I was born...and all that David Copperfield kind of crap, but I don't feel like going into it."

Sex, drugs, and violence fueled much of the edgy language of the 1960s and 1970s, when no-holds-barred writers like William Burroughs, Hunter S. Thompson, and Charles Bukowski reigned supreme. And Kathy Acker took that language to its post-punk, feminist, in-your-face extreme.

But editors say they are wearying of shock for shock's sake, even if media producers are not. Today's paragons of edgy literary prose are likely to be found overseas among novelists like Will Self and Martin Amis. In Amis's *Yellow Dog,* even inanimate objects shudder into nervous coexistence with his protagonists: Toenails give a "defiant tick" when lopped; fireplace logs expectorate and regurgitate. And in the air, a plane

> revealed her silver breast to the sun. As she rose, a cross-wind jolted her fiercely to starboard; a beast of the upper air had tried to seize her, and then let her slip from his grasp like a bar of soap.

EDGY LANGUAGE AND STYLE

Some misconceptions surround the term *edgy language,* which is often confused with runaway obscenity. But foul-mouthing is just one type of edgy locution—the easiest to execute, yet, as evidenced by many a 'zine or blog, prone to being pointless and edgeless. Obscenity works best when its edge comes not from the naughtiness of the words, but, as in a David Mamet play, from the turmoil of its speakers.

Edgy language can perhaps be thought of as "words in turmoil." If the gross and obscene can be nerve-wrenching, so can conflicted grammar, agitated word order, strung-out usage, and psychotic metaphor. Sentences can be clipped or stretched into rhythms so manic and caffeinated they "make coffee nervous," to paraphrase writer/director Nora Ephron.

America's edgy stylists include Joan Didion, with her strings of tense one-line paragraphs, and David Foster Wallace, virtuoso of the damaged-psyche perspective (". . . something vaguely digestive about the room's odor." —*Infinite Jest*). Also in this circle is Don DeLillo—a writer, in the words of John Updike, whose "fervent intelligence and . . . fastidious, edgy prose weave halos of import around every event." Snippets of DeLillo's prose agitate my own notebooks. A sampling from *Cosmopolis:*

> The idea was to live outside the given limits, in a chip, on a disk, as data, in a whirl, in a radiant spin. . . . The technology was imminent or not. It was semi-mythical. It was the natural next step. It would never happen. It is happening now.

Novelist Chuck Palahniuk's fans have crowned him a prince of edge for a style that is, according to one reviewer, "equal parts potent imagery, nihilistic coolspeak, and doped-out craziness." In his gothic thriller *Diary,* a woman in psychic pain narrates the tale in clipped, tormented locutions addressed to her husband, who lies comatose after a failed suicide. Her bitter, second-person narration delivers close-up images as merciless as the anatomical zooms on TV's *CSI: Crime Scene Investigation:*

With your kind of coma victims, all the muscles contract. The tendons cinch in tighter and tighter. Your knees pull up to the chest. Your arms fold in, close to your gut. Your feet, the calves contract until the toes point screaming straight down, painful to even look at. . . . Just so you know how bad you look, any person in a coma longer than two weeks, doctors call this a persistent vegetative state. Your face swells and turns red. Your teeth start to drop out.

One or two passages may not convey the edge created by language; more often the effect is cumulative. Nor does everyone agree on who or what is edgy. Like other art qualities, edge exists in the eye of the beholder. "I know it when I see it" is how a Supreme Court justice once characterized obscenity, prompting wags to conclude that obscenity is "whatever excites a judge." And so with edge: whatever waggles one's ganglia.

EDGE AND YOU

WHAT IS EDGY WRITING?

Prose or poetry that features nervously stimulating content, action, language, or style.

WHO NEEDS IT?

Readers who like the rush of brinkmanship. Editors expected to deliver edgy content. Writers attuned to the aesthetic of edge or who crave the label *edgy* as a means of advancing their careers.

WHAT IS EDGY LANGUAGE?

Not just graphic and obscene words, but language at the nervous boundaries of grammar, syntax, and usage; of taste, of familiar vocabulary, of moral and legal risk.

HOW CAN I MAKE MY LANGUAGE MORE EDGY?

Read some of the edgy writers mentioned in this chapter and catch the fever. Shake up sentence length and rhythm. Unleash an attitude. Push vocabulary to daredevil extremes. Startle by what isn't said. Write neurotic passages—i.e., unpredictable, disjointed, repetitive, contradictory, heretical, offensive, freakishly metaphoric. Then step back. Did you evoke nervousness—or merely a soul-shattering cringe?

Keep trying. If edge came easy it would, well, lose its edge, wouldn't it?

EDGE CONTROL

Like knife throwers, we want our daggers to frame the live target, not puncture it. Or maybe graze an earlobe. The secret of writing edgy is to control what appears to be out of control. A vial of laudanum did not a Coleridge's "Kubla Khan" make; what made it—and made it edgy—was the poet steering readers through his phantasmagoria.

Edge is best when it appears to be driven by a credible force. When obviously contrived, it can come off like scripted reality TV. But of course writing *is* scripted. Edge-masters create the illusion of unpredictability, as if some I don't-know-what-I'll-say-next madness forces their hands.

[248]

And during the writing process, one may well *not* know what madness lies ahead. Artistic control comes in the editing, which should shape, not inhibit, any good stuff born of turmoil and a touch of lunacy.

Some developing writers feel uncomfortable showing their edgiest sides to the world. It may seem like self-exposure, even exhibitionism; and to the extent that artists cannot separate themselves from their creations, it is in fact a little of both. But one *can* distance the artist-self from the non-artist self, letting the one burst out in its most unpredictable nakedness, while the other goes quietly about its business. Call it the courage to write, or a functionally split personality, but this is a mind-set that writers usually develop as they write and publish—discovering that the private person remains intact. It is the mind-set that enables actors to play horrific characters, or comedians to turn themselves inside out before a live audience and be whole again in the morning.

The edgy comic David Chappelle said this to a *New York Times* reporter: "I'm not trying to push people's buttons. But at the same time . . . I don't want to hold back. Our [modus operandi] . . . is to dance like nobody's watching."

Mazurka, anyone?

THIRTY-ONE
PARTING WORDS: BUTTERFLIES IN THE KILLING FIELDS

Author Martin Amis, you might guess by now, is among those who come to mind when I contemplate my *Spunk & Bite* Hall of Fame. And whenever Amis comes to mind, so does the cheery view of the cosmos expressed in *The Information,* his novel about competing writers: "[I]t would seem the universe is thirty billion light years across and every inch of it would kill us if we went there. This is the position of the universe with regard to life."

Amis, of course, lives in the literary world, that particularly lethal corner of the murderous universe. Here, too, every inch seems determined to kill—in this case, aspiring writers; tens of thousands of writers, all shooting for the stars, most of them careening back to earth, egos charred if not vaporized.

Take away the novas occupied by celebrity and brand-name authors, by troubadours of the sensational and schlocky, and the universe can be very dark indeed for writers. See them wandering in the void: writing-program grads with promising portfolios; bloggers pouring out their souls to phantom readers; journalers laboring in the interstices between kids and sleep. So many writers. So many good writers. So few places in the stingy publishing firmament.

And yet, hallowed places are reserved for writers possessed of just two assets: something remarkable to say to a paying crowd, and the language—the expressive style—to leave competing writers in the cosmic dust.

But does language still matter in this supposedly dumbed-down world? Of course it does. It will matter until people stop using words to symbolize everything that stimulates them. *Brilliant* language, however, matters less in writing if you happen to be, say, an author named Donald Trump, or if you've chewed off a limb to escape enemy captors and lived to tell about it, or if your miracle diet has diminished someone's celebrated booty.

Also, if theme, plot, or characterization propels your fiction beyond the Van Allen Belt, then perhaps language and style can simply tag along for the ride. But in the history of storytelling, has anything roused souls and stirred juices more than the well-chosen word? Almost always, you will rise above the crowd, or be lost in it, based on how you use language.

RISING FROM THE SLUSH

Most editors become editors because of a special infatuation with language. As they review manuscripts and proposals, they must first consider theme (or topic) and its appeal to an audience, and then how well that theme is treated. But the themes they see, submitted time after time, can be categorized within several weary types. And while a number of the treatments are competent, they, too, take on a certain sameness after a while. Heads will jerk up at novel themes or concussively fresh approaches, but these are rare.

More reliably, all else being equal, the masterly, distinctive use of language lifts an editor's (or agent's) heart. It means that the writing, as is, will please critics; that it will deliver on a promise to readers. Exciting language can elevate manuscripts from the slush heaps to that rarefied level known as "serious considera-

[251]

tion." And when serious contenders vie for publication, again it is language—spunky, biting, or coruscating language—that can "pierce the empyrean and make the welkin ring," as a wordsmith once wrote of a New York skyscraper.

Language boosts one effort above the other even among works distinguished by, say, an ingenious plot or a controversial or compelling topic, such as a breakthrough in science. Language establishes the engaging personality and point of view of narrator or character, yields voices that connect with the reader. It allows the bland to sound grand, and the grand to sound as grand as when Johannes Kepler exulted over his new harmonic law (the third law of planetary motion): "Now . . . a very few days after the pure Sun of that most wonderful study began to shine, nothing restrains me; it is my pleasure to yield to the sacred frenzy."

FRENZY AND RESTRAINT

Given the leg-up importance of language, a writer has to ask: How can I sparkle? How do I rise to the next level? How do I beat out the others? I have offered my thoughts in the previous chapters, but at one point you the writer will have to yield to your own sacred frenzy; charge like some mad lepidopterist through the meadows of language—every kind of meadow—and net the butterflies, let them loose in your pages.

The great Vladimir Nabokov literally chased butterflies in the fields of Europe and New York State, and, perhaps inspired, wrote sentence upon sentence that fluttered in a golden light. But like so many master stylists, Nabokov walked a thin line between splendor and excess. The language called attention to itself. It indulged in erudite wordplay. It showed off, grew elephantine. It might have been too much had he not directed it, like a mahout guiding his pachyderm, to the service of story and characterization.

When virtuosity of language and style starts to overwhelm story (or, in nonfiction, the point), it is time to tug at the reins. But writers often rein themselves in from the start, never giving sacred frenzy a chance. And little wonder: There are as many pressures to write cautiously as to protect hearth and home, to avoid strangers and heed orange alerts. As Sinclair Lewis said, "every compulsion is put upon writers to become safe, polite, obedient, and sterile."

We all know those compulsions, whether inspired by audience, employers, the national frame of mind, or one's own anxieties. From within come fears of derision by peers and critics; of exposure as a know-nothing bungler of the language; of shame brought upon friends and family; of general censure and censorship, of Big Brother.

Writing has always been about surmounting fears. But at the end of the day—at the beginning, too—only a single fear, that of *boring your readers,* merits a change in the direction of one's language and style. Given today's competition for reader attention, that change will likely be in the direction of excess—inventive, artful excess, but well outside the safety net. To go there takes courage. Where does it come from? From the nobility of the mission: To refresh readers from the fug of the ordinary, the numbing, and the nurturing. Writer, it is your *duty* to do so!

And if occasionally you land on your tokus, that is only the journey, the way, of spunk and bite. To stand out from the crowd, one goes for broke, one wins, one loses, one learns, one survives. What is it that the protagonist of Philip Roth's *American Pastoral* declares about writing in general? "As pathological phenomena go, it doesn't *completely* wreck your life."

Spunky.

INDEX

A

Ackerman, Diane, 31, 135, 179
adjectives, 34, 42, 121
adverbs, 121; defined, 37; examples to match-up, 40; functions, 38; lively uses, 37–42; of degree, 39; of manner, 39; stylish '-ly' type, 39–42; worn-out, 42
Alaska Quarterly Review, 182
Ali, Muhammad, 62
Alighieri, Dante, 235, 244
Allen, Woody, 10
Allred, Mike, 81
American Literary Review, 183
Amis, Martin, 30, 63, 107, 130, 245, 251
Ammons, A. R., 166
Anderson, John Lee, 169
ARTFL Project: Roget's Thesaurus (Web site), 76
audience: and diction, 55; contemporary, 2, 237. *SEE ALSO* GENERATIONS, WRITING FOR VARIOUS
Augustine, Saint, 131
avant-gardism, differing from edge, 243

B

Banville, John, 69
Barry, Dave, 68, 139
Bartlett's Roget's Thesaurus (1996), 75
Beard, Henry, 41
Binchy, Maeve, 111
Bling (Kennedy), 232
bloggers and blogging, 87, 118, 230, 251
Blythe, Will, 21, 42
borrowings. *SEE* FOREIGNISMS
Brooks, David, 67, 88
Brown, Sandra, 111
Browning, Robert, 80
Bryson, Bill, 14, 64, 168, 178, 210
Buchanan, Edna, 133
Buckley, William F. Jr., 98
Budd, Malcolm, 217
Byrne, Elena Karina, 117

C

Camus, Albert, 245
Carson, Rachel, 135
Cary, Joyce, 48

[255]

catacosmesis, 13

Cerf, Chris, 41

Chabon, Michael, 32, 33

Chandler, Raymond, 68

Chapelle, David, 249

ch'i, as force in writing, 188–195. *SEE ALSO* FENG SHUI

chick lit, 67

Cisneros, Sandra, 32, 34, 56, 160

Clark, Mary Higgins, 111

closings, 140–146; cliché, 144; conventional models, 142–144; do's and do not's, 145; importance of, 140; strategies, 141; summational, 142

Coetzee, J. M., 70

coinages. *SEE* NEOLOGISMS

Collins, Billy, 124

colon, 174

color: describing, 30–36; examples of inventive use, 32; intensifying, 33

comedy: in coinages, 90; in openings, 139; via pop references, 236; with hyphenated modifiers, 152. *SEE ALSO* TROPES (figures of speech)

comma, 154, 174, 177

competing as a writer, vii, 2, 6–7, 251–253; importance of language in, 252–253; inhibiting fears, 254

conceits, 69

Conrad, Barnaby, 112

Cooper, Ilene, 233

copywriters and copywriting, vii, 7, 87, 201

Corbeil, Jean-Claude, 211

Cornwell, Patricia, 111

correctness, 5

cummings, e. e., 83

Cunnah, Michelle, 51

D

D'Ambrosio, Charles, 60

D'Angelo, Mike, 15, 117, 236

Daily, Janet, 111

Daly, Steve, 150

dangling modifiers, 196–204; with delayed subjects, 199; with infinitive phrases, 201; and possessives, 199; examples, 200–201; hunting for, 198, 199; test for, 200; when acceptable, 202–203

dash, 174

Day, Price, 136

De Botton, Alain, 32

Definition a Day, A (Web site), 27

DeLillo, Don, 15, 50, 82, 246

Denby, David, 66

Describer's Dictionary: A Treasury of Terms and Literary Quotations, The (Grambs), 209

description: in lists, 164; of named things, 205–212; of color, 30–36; of the extremely great or small, 16–22; using pop imagery, 234–241; using sound imagery, 80–85; using tropes, 61–70

Descriptionary: A Thematic Dictionary (McCutcheon), 209

dialogue: alternative styles, 180–186; diction, 58; foreign words in, 98; hyphenated modifiers in, 151–152; of Generation Y, 230; sentence fragments in, 155; semicolons in, 176; using enallage, 117. *SEE ALSO* DIALOGUE ATTRIBUTION (tagging)

dialogue attribution (tagging), 106–112; alternative styles, 180–186; avoiding "swifties," other pitfalls, 108; dramatic style, 108;

examples of zesty, 110; foreign words in, 99; lean style, 107; virtues of extravagant, 110. SEE ALSO DIALOGUE

Diaz, Juno, 14

Dickens, Charles, 159

diction, 53–60; acquiring personal, 54; and audience, 55; elements of, 59; high and low, 55; poetic, 58; pointers in applying, 58; purpose in written works, 53; types, 54; unexpected, 14, 57

Didion, Joan, 157, 246

Dowd, Maureen, 15, 97, 150, 236

Dybek, Stuart, 46

E

Eats, Shoots & Leaves (Truss), 57, 62, 171

echoic effects, 81

edge, 242–249; and ephemera, 240; and language, 245; controlling, 248; defined, 243; dynamics of, 243; history in literature, 244–245; obscenity, 245–246; pocket guide to, 247

edgy writing. SEE EDGE

Eggers, Dave, 124, 161

Elements of Style, The (Strunk and White), viii, 2–8, 94, 122, 124, 195

Elkin, Stanley, 103

Ellison, Ralph, 32

Emerson, Ralph Waldo, 222

enallage, 13, 113–119; defined, 113; *disconnect* (noun) as example of, 115; dynamics of, 114–115; functional labels, 114; in jargon, 118; uses of, 116

English Primrose, The (Hodges), 171

endings. SEE CLOSINGS

ephemeragy (ephemeral imagery), 234–241; defined, 235

F

fears, overcoming, 101, 249, 253

feng shui: applied to sentences, 190; checklist for editing, 194; "cures" for bad writing, 193; defined, 189; of writing, 187–195; yin and yang in, 189

figures of speech. SEE TROPES, AND UNDER TYPE: E.G., CATACOSMESIS, ENALLAGE, HYPERBOLE, METAPHOR, SIMILE, ONOMATOPOEIA, OXYMORON

Fiske, Robert Hartwell, 63

Fitch, Janet, 32, 70, 216

Flesch, Rudolph, 149

Foer, Jonathan Safran, 21

Follett, Wilson, 101, 149, 214

Forché, 33

foreignisms, 93–104; arguments against, 95, 99; options, 94; reasons to use, 96; style rules, 96; suggested terms, 102

Fowler, H. W., 95, 149

Frank, Anne, 129

Franzen, Jonathan, 24, 34, 166, 214

Frazier, Charles, 185

Frere-Jones, Sasha, 66

Friedan, Betty, 132

functional shifts or variations. SEE ENALLAGE

Furst, Alan, 78

G

Galleano, Eduardo, 53

Garcia, Eric, 66

Garg, Aru, 28

Garner, Bryan, 114

Garner's Modern American Usage (Garner), 114

generations, writing for various, 224–233; Baby Boomers, 224, 225 (defined); 229; commonalities, 232–233; false labels, 228; fine-tuning to, 232; "generation," definition and influences of, 227–228; Generation X, 224, 226 (defined); Generation Y, 224, 227 (defined), 229; Generation Z, 224, 227 (defined); keeping current with, 231; mimicking, 230; patterns, 229; publishers' attitudes, 224

Germanisms. SEE HYPHENATED MODIFIERS

Glatt, Lisa, 66

Glazier, Stephen, 208

Gogh, Vincent van, on color, 30

Gomer, Peter, 134

Gopnik, Adam, 151

Gordimer, Nadine, 81

Gudding, Gabriel, 83

H

Haddon, Mark, 58

Haley, Alex, 132

Hall, Richard, 90

Hammett, Dashiell, 65

Harrison, Jim, 33

Harvard Review, 182

Hemingway, Ernest, 138

Herr, Michael, 135

Hijuelos, Oscar, 192

Hitchens, Christopher, 20

Holmes, Shannon, 56

hyperbole, 17, 61

hyphen, 154

hyphenated modifiers, 148–154; charms of, 151; criticism of, 149; examples, 150; in dialogue, 151; rules of, 153

I

I Am Charlotte Simmons (Wolfe), 231

I Ching (Book of Changes), 188

imagery, 16; color, 30–36; megaphors, 16–17; miniphors, 16, 19; pop, 234–241; sound, 80–85; surprising, 10

immediacy, 45

indirection, 13

intensifiers, 120–126; defined, 120; everyday, 121; frequency study, 123; historic, 121; in poetry, 124; stock, value of, 122; when to avoid, 125

intensity. SEE INTENSIFIERS

Internet: as vocabulary source, 27; thesauruses on, 76

Irving, John, 88, 111, 173

Ishiguro, Kazuo, 59

J

Jackson, Renay, 56

jargon, 118

Journalism, New, 7, 141

journalists and journalism: coinages, 87; enallage, 114; endings, 140–146; extreme metaphors, 17; foreign terms, 97; immediacy, 45; intensifiers, 123; leads, 127–139; participial phrases, 198; semicolons, 173; sentence fragments, 160; tropes, 62; going for edge, 242; use of pop references, 235

Joyce, James, 181

K

Kakutani, Michiko, 38
Kantor, McKinley, 181
Kaplan, Janice, 67
Karasyov, Carrie, 64
Kargman, Jill, 64
Karon, Jan, 111
Kellerman, Jonathan, 11
Kelman, James, 59
Kennedy, Erica, 232
Kennedy, William, 50, 169
Kepler, Johannes, 253
Kerouac, Jack, 245
Kis, Danilo, 164
Klein, Lee, 118

L

Lanchester, John, 60
leads. *SEE* OPENINGS
Lee, Andrea, 167
Lehane, Dennis, 150
Lent, Jeffrey, 217
Leonard, Elmore, 106
Lewis, Sinclair, 254
Leyner, Mark, 152, 167, 234, 236–237, 240
libraries, 74, 208
lists, creative, 163–170; art of, 164; examples (food items), 168; ideal length, 167; mechanics of, 169; poetic qualities, 166; symbolic elements, 165
loanwords, 94
locution, defined, 8

Longinus, Cassius, 68
Lopez, Barry, 35
Lyon, Jeff, 134

M

Martel, Yann, 161
Maslin, Janet, 63
Mason, Daniel, 50
McCaffery, Larry, 240
McCarthy, Cormac, 185, 217
McEwan, Ian, 67
Meehan, William, 98
megaphors. *SEE UNDER* IMAGERY
Melville, Herman, 158
Merriam-Webster's Word of the Day (Web site), 27
metaphor: conceits, 69; defined, 63; extreme, 16; extreme (examples of), 20; for colors, 33–34. *SEE ALSO* TROPES (figures of speech)
metonymy, 14
miniphors. *SEE UNDER* IMAGERY
Mister Johnson (Cary), 48
Mitchell, Elvis, 65, 237
Moby Dick (Melville), 158
Modern American Usage (Follett), 203
modifiers. *SEE* ADJECTIVES; ADVERBS; DANGLING MODIFIERS; HYPHENATED MODIFIERS; INTENSIFIERS
Morrison, Toni, 175, 176, 179
Mosley, Walter, 63
Mukherjee, Bharati, 168

N

Nabokov, Vladimir, 103, 111, 163, 253
names (of things). *SEE* NOMENCLATURE

neologisms, 13, 86–92; and enallage, 117; as entertainment, 90; defined, 87; duration, 90; for writing matters (exercise), 88; forming, 90; purposes, 87

New York Times, The: and stylish adverbs, 38; dangling participles, 196, 199. *SEE ALSO UNDER SPECIFIC STAFF WRITERS*

Newlove, David, 160

Nickels, Harry G., 124

nomenclature: aptness, 210; precise, 205–212; exercise, 206; in visual dictionaries, 211; poetic, 211; reference sources, 205, 207–208

O

O'Hanlon, Redmond, 32, 84

Oates, Joyce Carol, 21

Official Politically Correct Dictionary and Handbook (Beard and Cerf), 41

Oliver, Mary, 69

On Great Writing (Longinus), 69

On Writing (King), 73, 107

onomatopoeia, 211; cliché, 82; defined, 80; examples (sounds of spring), 83; in casual use, 81; in comics, 81; theories of, 82; using, 80–85

openings, 127–139; as stimulation, 127; cliché 136; comedic, 139; first- and second-person, 135; invitational, 137; literary, 138; promises contained in, 128; sincerity in, 131; strategies, 129; style elements, 129; touching on sensibilities, 132; types of, 133; using quotations in, 136

Oxford Dictionary of Foreign Words and Phrases, The (1997), 101

oxymoron, 13, 39

Ozick, Cynthia, 225

P

Packer, Z. Z., 244

Paine, Thomas, 131

Palahniuk, Chuck, 246

Palliser, Charles, 111

Pappademas, Alex, 66

paragraph breaks, in dialogue, 185

parataxis, 176

participial phrases: beauty of, 198; defined, 197

participles: defined, 197. *SEE ALSO* DANGLING MODIFIERS

particulars, nomenclature of, 205–212. *SEE ALSO* LISTS, CREATIVE; NOMENCLATURE

period (punctuation mark), 174

personification, 13

phonesthemic word groups, 84

phonesthesia, 84;

Poe, Edgar Allan, 82, 88

Poniewozik, James, 150

pop: cultural status of, 240; defined, 234; exploitative, 240; facile, 241; images and references, 234–241; shelf-life of, 18, 237; tracking on the Web, 239

Pope, Alexander, 82

prefixes: in neologisms, 91; for augmenting, 21

Primary Colors (Theroux), 31

Proulx, E. Annie, 15, 20, 168, 207

Proverbs 8:30, 198

Pullman, Philip, 56

punctuation. *SEE* COLON; COMMA; DASH; HYPHEN; PERIOD; SEMICOLON; QUOTATION MARKS

puns, 62, 108

Pynchon, Thomas, 84

INDEX

Q

quotation marks: and semicolon, 177; importance in narration, 184; omitted in dialogue, 180–186

quoteless dialogue, 180–186; literary editors' views of, 182; useful effects, 185

R

Raab, Scott, 128

Random House Webster's College Thesaurus (1997–1998), 75

Random House Webster's Word Menu (Glazier), 208

rap, vocabulary of, 26

Ratliff, Ben, 15

really, 123

Reilly, Rick, 20, 67

rhetorical devices (for surprise), 13

Rice, Grantland, 134

Roberts, Selena, 15, 20

Robinson, Paul, 175

Roget, Peter, 73

Roget's (thesaurus), 72–79

Roget's International Thesaurus (1992, 2001), 75

Roget's Thesaurus of English Words and Phrases (1852), 72

Roth, Philip, 153, 157, 253

Rowling, J. K., 31, 87, 109

Rushdie, Salman, 20, 61, 110, 150

Russo, Richard, 241

S

Salinger, J. D., 245

Saramago, José, 184

Schnumberger, Lynn, 67

Schweser, Jamie, 150

Sebold, Alice, 66

Secondary Colors (Theroux), 31

Sedaris, David, 50, 236

Self, Will, 12, 37, 150, 243

Selzer, Richard, 139

semicolon, 171–179; and quotation marks, 177; art of, 172; as best option, 174; before conjunctions, 177; between single words, 176; conventional uses, 178; creating expectation, 175; history, 173; nuances of, 176 optional uses, 178

sentence fragments, 155–62; compared with full sentences, 158; in literature, 159; in poetry, 157; justification for, 155; pitfalls of, 156

sentences: common flaws and their fixes, 217–221; controlled, 214; engaging, 213–222; examples of faulty, 216; feng shui applied to, 190; judging by ear, 215; linking, 173; mantra for, 215; tasks of, 213. *SEE ALSO* SENTENCE FRAGMENTS; DANGLING MODIFIERS

Shakespeare, William, 86, 87, 118, 124, 173, 203, 244

Shields, Carol, 192

Shreve, Anita, 214

Shteyngart, Gary, 32

simile, 61, 63 (defined)

Singer, Mark, 190

Smiley, Jane, 15

Smith, Claire, 20

Smith, Graham, 54

Smith, Lee, 59

Smith, Zadie, 244

Sniglets (Hall), 90

so, as intensifier, 123–124, 127–128

Sontag, Susan, 50

Soukhanov, Anne H., 26

Souljah, Sister, 56

sound symbolism, 80, 83

sounds, imitative. *See* ONOMATOPOEIA

Sparks, Nicholas, 111

Spatz, Ronald, 182

Specter, Michael, 20

Spin magazine, 229

Spizzerinctum Obscure Words (Web site), 28

Steel, Danielle, 109

Stella, Leslie, 13, 236

Steyn, Mark, 20

stream-of-consciousness, 181

Strunk, William Jr., 2–6

Styron, William, 99

suffixes: in neologisms, 91; for augmenting or diminishing, 30

Surowiecki, James, 97

surprise, 10–15; devices for achieving, 13; sample uses of, 14

Swifties, 108

synecdoche, 14

synonyms: dictionaries of, 74; false, 72

T

tags, dialogue, 106–112; action, 112. *See also* DIALOGUE ATTRIBUTION (tagging)

Tait, John, 183

Tartt, Donna, 66, 103, 217

Tennyson, Alfred Lord, 80

tense: and genre, 51; base, 46; choosing, 44–52; for earlier and later action, 47; historical present, 46; immediacy, 45; in flashbacks, 47; in poetry, 51; modern uses of present, 47–58; modern uses of present (examples), 50; past and present compared, 45

Teutonicisms. *See* HYPHENATED MODIFIERS

Theroux, Alexander, 31, 111

Theroux, Paul, 103, 137

thesaurus: 19, 112; advantages of, 74; bundled, 73; limitations, 77; optimal use, 72–79; recommended editions, 74; *Roget's*, 72; tips for using, 77; Web editions, 76

Thomas, Lewis, 175

Thompson, Christina, 182

Thurber, James, 81, 111

Time magazine, 141

tropes (figures of speech): 61–70; and texture, 70; as author entertainment, 64; comedic, 67–68; comparative, 63; evaluating, 64; excessive, 69; in poetry, 69; in prose vs. poetry, 62; qualities of good, 63

Truss, Lynne, 57, 62, 138, 171, 173

Tyangiel, Josh, 68

U

umami, defined, 93

understatement, 13, 21, 129, 245

Updike, John, 31, 134

Urdang, Lawrence, 24

usage, 77, 86, 114; and diction, 54, 59; descriptivists vs. prescriptivists, 4; foreign borrowings, 96; hyphenated modifiers, 153

V

Vargas Llosa, Mario, 165

Verigin, Lisa, 242

very, 123

visual dictionaries, 211

Visual Thesaurus, The (Web site), 76

INDEX

vocabulary. *SEE* WORDS

Vocabulary Word of the Day, The (Web site), 27

W

Wallace, David Foster, 175, 218, 246

Wallraff, Barbara, 90

Webster's New World Roget's A–Z Thesaurus (1999), 76

Weldon, Fay, 67, 110, 217, 241

White, E. B. (Elwyn Brooks), 2–8, 124

Whitman, Walt, 198

Wilde, Oscar, 107

Wilson, Robert, 103

Winchester, Simon, 72

Wines, Michael, 15

Wired Style: Principles of English Usage in the Digital Age (Hale), 149

Wolfe, Tom, 8, 81, 82, 130, 149, 231

Word a Day, A (Web site), 27

word choice. *SEE* DICTION

Word of the Day (Web site), 27

Word Spy, The (Web site), 27

words: adding to vocabulary, 23–29; nomenclature, 210; best sources of, 26; foreign, 93–104; from Internet sites, 27; in thesauruses, 77; intensifying, 120–126; number of in English, 86; qualities of "writers' words", 25; techniques for coining, 90; using unfamiliar, 25, 29

Wordsmyth Dictionary-Thesaurus (Web site), 76

Wordsworth, William, 87, 177

Worthless Word for the Day (Web site), 27

Y

yin and yang. *SEE UNDER* FENG SHUI

Z

Zinsser, William, 135, 145

6/06